I0004370

Architecting Big Data & Analytics Solutions - Integrated with IoT & Cloud

Create strategic business insights with agility

Dr Mehmet Yildiz

Distinguished Enterprise Architect

Third Edition, Revised and Re-edited, October 2019

Copyright © Dr Mehmet Yildiz

Author Contact: https://digitalmehmet.com

Publisher: S.T.E.P.S. Publishing Australia

P.O Box 2097, Roxburgh Park, Victoria, 3064 Australia

info@stepsconsulting.com.au

Edited by Stephen Barkly

Disclaimer

Table of Contents

Introduction

Purpose of this book

IoT, Big Data Analytics, and Cloud Computing are three distinct technology domains with overlapping use cases. Each technology has its own merits; however, the combination of three creates a synergy and the golden opportunity for businesses to reap the exponential benefits. This combination can create technological magic for innovation when adequately architected, designed, implemented, and operated.

Integrating Big Data with IoT and Cloud architectures provide substantial business benefits. It is like a perfect match. IoT collects real-time data using smart objects. Big Data optimises data management solutions. Cloud collects, hosts, computes, stores, and disseminates data rapidly.

Based on these compelling functions and business propositions, the primary purpose of this book is to provide practical guidance on creating Big Data solutions integrated with IoT and Cloud service models. To this end, the book offers an architectural overview, solution practice, governance, and underlying technical approach for creating integrated Big Data, Cloud, and IoT solutions.

The book offers an introduction to the process of solution architecture, three distinct chapters comprising Big Data, Cloud, and the IoT with the final chapter, including conclusive remarks to consider for Big Data solutions. These chapters include essential architectural points, solution practice, methodical rigour, techniques, technologies, and relevant tools.

Creating Big Data solutions are complex and complicated from multiple angles. However, with the awareness and guidance provided in this book, the Big Data solutions architects can be empowered to provide useful and productive solutions with growing confidence.

Audience

This book has a specific focus on Big Data solution architects; however, its content can be an interest in all types of architects in Big Data, IoT, and Cloud Computing areas.

Apart from architects, this book can provide useful insights to senior technical leaders such as CTOs (Chief Technology Officers), CDO (Chief Digital Officers), Chief Data Officers, and CIOs (Chief Information Officers) to understand the architectural considerations for these critical technologies ubiquitously taking over the Information Technology Services globally.

This book can also be useful for the advanced tertiary students planning a career in these growing technology areas, understand the best practices, and see the big picture for their desired professions reflected from practice al work settings.

Summary of Chapters

Chapter 1:

Architectural Solution Process

This chapter provides an overview of the architectural solution process by introducing the critical solution work-products.

Chapter 2:

IoT, Big Data and Cloud Relationships

This chapter provides a high-level view of these technologies (IoT, Big Data, Cloud) setting the architectural framework by defining them from architectural perspectives. It provides an overview of relationships for these three distinct technologies in terms of creating the synergies and potential benefits for business with an agile approach.

Chapter 3:

Big Data Architecture Process

This core chapter provides Big Data architectural solutions, providing an overview of the process, technologies, methods, and tools.

Chapter 4:

Cloud for Big Data

This chapter provides an overview of Cloud Computing architecture and solutions related to Big Data solutions. It provides an overview of the process, technologies, methods, and tools.

Chapter 5:

IoT for Big Data

This chapter is dedicated to IoT architecture and solutions, providing an overview of the process, technologies, methods, and tools within the context of Big Data.

Chapter 6:

Conclusions

This chapter, to bring all together, provides conclusive remarks and critical considerations for the use of IoT and Cloud Computing services for Big Data solutions.

Chapter 1: Architectural Solution Process

Purpose of this Chapter

Before starting the significant themes of the book, in this section, we have an overview and a high-level walkthrough of the primary architectural tasks for creating Big Data solutions. Experienced solution architects may skip this section. However, it can be useful to have a quick scan of the common work-products covered in this chapter.

Understanding the context is vital for solution architects. Therefore, this section sets the context for the solution architecture process. By understanding the context, we can have a common understanding of what an architectural solution means and what it covers.

In this section, we touch on general architectural practice and knowledge. This practice can be transferred or applied to any architectural solutions. They are not just unique to Big Data solutions.

The view I provide here depicts only fundamental aspects and covers very condensed content to start the solution journey. Those who are starting solution architecture practice, I'd recommend undertaking an architectural method course which can provide a comprehensive and an end to end view. Learning the purpose and content of the solution work-products are essential for any architects. Otherwise, it can be difficult, messy, and time-consuming to produce desired results.

Without further ado, let's start by presenting an overview of the fundamental architectural approach for creating solutions. Architectural tasks are covered under the name of 'solution work-products'. Architectural methods also call these tasks 'work-products'.

Solution Work-Products

A work-product is an essential term used in architectural vernacular. Work-products are standard terms in the industry. Solution architects create and deal with multiple architectural work-products.

These work-products are template documents that prompt the solution architects to enter the required information with guiding notes. Work-product templates are created based on experience and lessons learned from previous successful projects. There can be many work-products for a specified solution.

The standard view of work-products in an organisation can save time to the architects, reviewers, specialists, and other content contributors from various domains. Many organisations have their mandatory work-products used for solution architectures in their method. Let's understand what an architectural method is.

Architectural Solution Method

An architectural method is a step by step guide to complete a solution providing templates, solution building blocks, techniques, annotations, and references.

To create solution architectures, rather than proverbial re-inventing the wheel, we can follow an established method to save time. Following an established method allows solution architects to achieve predictable and repeatable results. These methods have evolved through their multiple uses. In turn, the techniques covered in these methods have also evolved through the reuse of successful implementations, as well as the lessons learnt from failed projects.

There can be hundreds of work-products in sophisticated solution methods. To keep it concise and see the big picture, we only focus on the primary work-products, that matter, related to our solution scope. Please keep in mind that your organisation may mandate more work-products to comply with the solution delivery requirements. If your organisation is a service provider, your customers may also have their proprietary method which you need to use to create your solutions. To further complicate the situation, your organisation may mandate some work-products in your method, and your customer organisation may mandate additional work-products in their method. As solution architects, we need to be flexible to meet methodical requirements for both stakeholders.

Strategy and Architectural Thinking

An architectural solution starts with strategic thinking. The architectural strategy takes place at the beginning of a solution. Setting the strategy upfront help the solution team to understand where they are now and where they are going. With this strategic approach in mind, an established method can help us reach our destination most effectively. This means that setting the strategy and following the method are two essential tasks in the earlier phase of solution development.

The solution strategy process provides an objective assessment of the current situation. It aligns project goals with the organisational goals and ensures that all gaps are covered. The solution strategy document also includes the opportunities, threats, strengths and weaknesses of the project from the technical, commercial and financial angles.

We know that the strategy of a solution hardly changes in the later phases of the solution process. Therefore, it must be understood and approved at earlier phases. However, we can make our strategy flexible by creating changeable tactics to empower our solution strategy. These tactics can also be documented and approved as part of the solution architecture approval process.

As solution architects, we ask substantial questions leading towards finding solution answers. One of the critical questions we ask is where we are now, where we are going as our target, and how to go there. This approach implies understanding the current environment, setting up the future environment, and creating a pathway and relevant mechanisms to move from the current sate to the future state. This is the most fundamental task of a high-level solution architect.

Architectural thinking is a process reflected by the day-to-day activities of the solution architects. This type of thinking is also facilitated by following an established method which serves the purpose of a map for the target solution architecture. Architectural thinking also considers the functional and non-functional aspects of the solution.

Architectural thinking is an essential skill for any architect. Like methodical practitioners, solution architects start working on a brief by first understanding the requirements set by the client. Therefore, requirements analysis is a fundamental architectural activity.

Solution Requirements

Solution architects collect, create, process, and formulate the technical requirements based on the business requirements which come from the business analysts or business architects. Besides, we also review the technical requirements created by other technical and operational specialists.

A requirements analysis may take up to several days to weeks or months, depending on the complexity of the projects at hand. The requirements are put in a matrix and analysed systematically to ensure nothing falls into the cracks. Using an incremental approach to requirements processing can be useful and productive.

A structured approach to a requirements analysis helps architects to understand mandatory and optional requirements and how they are met with adequate justification. For this approach, we use a requirements traceability matrix. This matrix helps us to track the requirements once the solution is drafted. The requirements traceability process continues until the successful completion of the solution.

The lead solution architects need to understand the details of both the functional and non-functional aspect of the solution well. Functional and Non-Functional requirements are like inseparable Yin and Yang. They need to be analysed and documented in an integrated manner. Let's briefly define these two types of requirements and understand their nature.

The functional requirements of a solution involve what the system offers to the consumers as functionality to be accomplished. For example, the system may offer calculations, data processing, and workflows. These are usually related to the consumers of the solution.

Non-functional aspects involve how the system can accomplish these functionalities, such as performance, availability, security, reliability, scalability, usability, configuration, and so on. These are technical and operational requirements. The tasks involved in the Non-Functional requirements relate to the IT support and maintenance teams.

Requirements need to be SMART—an acronym we use to describe the quality of requirements. Using the SMART acronym, we can confirm that the requirements must be specific, measurable, actionable, realistic and traceable. A critical aspect to the requirements analyses is the use of the MoSCoW rule, as adopted from the following Agile methods: 1) must have requirements; 2) should have, if at all possible; 3) could have, but not critical; 4) will not have this time, but potentially later.

The requirements need to be reviewed, endorsed and approved by various stakeholders. Once the requirements are approved by a governance body in the organisation, the solution architects can then start other architectural activities in the lifecycle, such as setting the System Context.

Solution Use Cases

We must obtain, analyse, understand and validate the solution use cases. The validated use cases can be very beneficial for requirement validation and making architectural decisions. A use case is a specific situation in which a product or service of a solution to be used by the consumers. Use cases are developed from the users' perspective. We need to understand how the consumers are intended to be using a particular component or aspect of the solution. Usually, the functional requirements can help us to formulate the use cases; or, in some circumstances, use cases help formulate the Functional Requirements. This means that the use cases and requirements are interrelated. We need to analyse them together; not in isolation.

Some selected users can help us understand the use cases when we interact with them. We need to ask the users questions and obtain their feedback on how they are intended to use a function that is expected to be in the IoT solution document. In general, overall solution use cases need to be defined and elaborated with the input of all stakeholders of the solution, not just end-users. There may be different use cases for different stakeholders.

Use cases can also be determined based on the roles and personas involves in developing a solution. Personas represent fictitious characters, which are based on our knowledge of the users in the solution. Identifying personas and the use of them in our use case development and requirements analysis can be very beneficial. Once the use cases are understood, precisely documented, and approved by all the relevant stakeholders, the requirements can be more explicit, decisions can be made more effectively, and the solution building blocks can be developed with more confidence.

System Context

Based on understanding the requirements, the context (preferably presented as a diagram) can be used to show the entities and relationships of the solution components at the highest level.

The System Context helps the key stakeholders understand the solution as an end-to-end service or a system. The System Context is usually represented on a single page. It is an ideal communication tool for senior executives and business stakeholders to see the bigger picture of the solution.

The System Context is also beneficial for technical team members, project managers and any other stakeholders working on the solution. The System Context rarely changes once it is understood and approved.

Current Environment

Solution architects document, review and analyse the current environment. The Current Environment work-product includes the details of the hardware, software, operating systems, functionalities, service levels, operational status, and many other factors. This document can be very detailed. It can also have a master document linking various aspects of the current systems. Without understanding the current system, it is not feasible to define the future system.

Future Environment

Based on the context and requirements, the solution architects set the future environment. This future environment is also called the target environment in architectural vernacular. The target environment requires substantial foundational architectural thinking. Requirements must be crystal clear when defining the future environment. A comprehensive breadth of knowledge is essential for a solution architects to define the future state. To successfully define the future environment, solution architects need to consult subject matter experts (SMEs) to validate the solution building blocks mapped to specific requirements.

Transitional Environment

Solution architects also create a transitional environment which may take place between the current and target environments. This new environment is usually needed when a migration solution is produced.

Architectural Models

Based on the context, it can be useful to create a few primary architectural models. One of the most useful models is a Component Model for the solution. This can start at a high level and drill down to the individual components, subcomponents and even elements of the central system. Component Models can also be useful for other stakeholders in a technical and business capacity to understand the components of the system and the relationships between them.

Solution architects also create another useful work-product—the operational model, which can be both logical and physical. The operational model shows how the solution can operate before it is implemented. This work-product can be used to gain the confidence of financial sponsors and other key project stakeholders. The operational model work-product brings everyone onto the same page in terms of how the system can operate.

In addition to the Component and Operational Models, there may be other models that solution architects need to develop. Some of the other critical architectural models are the performance model, availability model, business continuity model, configuration model and the deployment model.

Solution Viability

Another primary architectural work-product is called Solution Viability. The Solution Viability work-product includes the critical architectural and technical issues, risks, dependencies and assumptions. Project managers usually conduct the project or overall program Viability Assessments. The Solution Architect needs to develop and maintain the architectural and technical Viability Assessments.

Viability Assessment work-product remains dynamic throughout the solution development lifecycle. However, it is not only simple assessment tool; it can also be used as a powerful communication tool for the key stakeholders of the solution who are interested in assessing the risks, issues and dependencies that might affect the solution.

Architectural Decisions

Architectural decisions are critical to solution architecture. These crucial decisions can have substantial implications for the success or failure of the solution. Some implications can be cost-related, while others can relate to performance, availability, security and scalability. We need to document architectural decisions upfront. These documented decisions must be approved by a governance body in the organisation. For micro-level designs, solution architects also need to document the design decisions and obtain approval at the program level. Design decisions usually have fewer implications than architectural decisions. However, design decisions are also important.

An architectural decision format includes the possible options, a description of the selected option and the rationale for the selected option with clear recommendations. These recommendations must be articulated in a way that all stakeholders understand the impact and implications of the selected option. Architectural Decisions documents must be clear, concise and verifiable. They are usually single-page documents.

It is critical that the architectural decisions for solutions need to be made carefully as each decision can have a severe impact once the solution is implemented, and the consumption process has started. The impact may be on cost, performance, and many other aspects of the solution. They can even determine the destiny of the project in terms of its success or failure. Let's bear in mind that if the architecture is wrong, then everything can go wrong.

Solution Trade-offs

Architectural solutions require making trade-offs to reach optimal solution outcomes. When making trade-offs, we need to consider critical factors, such as cost, quality, functionality, usability and many other non-functional items. A trade-off can be defined as creating a balance between two required yet incompatible items. In other words, a trade-off is a compromise between two options. It is possible to make a trade-off between quality and cost for particular items. Some of the architectural trade-offs are required to be made for dealing with uncertainties. For these types of trade-offs, techniques such as comparing, and contrasting can be beneficial.

Reference Architectures

A reference architecture is a re-usable solution or a design in a template format. The use of a reference architecture for IoT solutions can save us a considerable amount of time. Reference architectures are developed by experienced solution architects based on successful outcomes obtained from delivered solutions. This means that we can trust the reference architectures as they were once successfully delivered. Following the same path as our customised specifications, these re-usable templates can save us a considerable amount of time and can improve the quality of our solutions.

As reference architectures are developed by experienced architects, they can also guide us in dealing with the unknown aspects of the solutions. Reference architectures can be used for various domains, can be combined to extend functionality and can be integrated for the final architecture solutions. Some architects share their experiences for various reasons. For example, some architects share them for charitable give-back purposes or networking, or to boost their reputation and recognition in their industry. Whatever the reasons they share them, the reference architectures are invaluable resources for our planned solution architectures.

Open-source organisations produce many reference architectures in their domains. There are two primary sources for these reference architectures: either their members develop them as part of an open-source team, or some commercial companies donate their re-usable assets to the open-source organisations as reference architectures. The Open Group (TOG) is a typical example of this kind of open-source organisation.

Reference Architectures can be at a high-level or other detailed levels. A typical IoT reference Architecture at a high level can include critical points, such as Portal, Dashboard, API Management, Analytics, Services, Communications, Devices, Device Management, Security Management, Infrastructure and so on. Reference Architectures are usually represented in diagrams with minimal text to explain the representations in the diagrams. Clarity is the main factor for a reference architecture. Reference Architectures usually are easy to understand and use.

Now let's start discussing how we can apply this knowledge to produce Big Data solutions using IoT and Cloud services.

Chapter 2: Big Data, IoT & Cloud Computing Relationship

IoT, Big Data and Cloud Computing are three distinct technology domains with overlapping use cases. Each technology has its own merits; however, the combination of three creates a synergy and the golden opportunity for businesses to reap the exponential benefits. This combination can create technological magic for innovation when adequately architected, designed, implemented and operated.

We can start with a high-level view of these technologies, defining them from architectural perspectives and provide an overview of their relationships in creating the synergies and potential benefits for business.

Even though these three technologies are distinct and have their use cases, for the scope of this book, the priority order for this book is the Big Data. It is the core value for creating business value.

To identify the relationships amongst these three technologies, we can start with the IoT and Big Data relationship. In this book, I propose IoT as the input or source data for the Big Data solutions. Big Data includes many types of data sets; however, the IoT data is essential to create innovations, new insights, and new business opportunities.

You may ask where does the Cloud Computing fit in this magical combination. Cloud Computing presents enabling and empowering capabilities, not only as a hosting platform for the Big Data but also providing advanced processing and analytics in an economical, scalable, reliable and agile manner.

Another view for identifying relationships can be obtained by looking at IoT an enriching factor for Big Data and Cloud as empowering. With the contributions from IoT and Cloud, the Big Data can achieve unprecedented results for creating new businesses and growing existing ones.

Big Data solutions without Cloud can be costly and complicated due to infrastructure requirements for storage, process and analytics requirements. Not only the enormous volume of the Big Data but also other vital characteristics such as a variety of data sources, velocity (speed), the veracity of data and required value from data in motion makes it a very complex system.

Of course, the scope of the Cloud is much bigger than just supporting the Big Data. Most recently, Cloud computing covers every aspect of Information Technology. However, for the scope of this book, we only look at the Cloud Computing as an enabler and empowering factor of the Big Data. Other aspects of the Cloud are beyond the scope of this book. There are myriad of books, and various other publications available on other aspects of the cloud on the market.

When we are creating the Big Data architecture solutions, it is critical to consider integrating IoT and Cloud to our solutions. IoT provides real-time data created by many sensors and smart objects used in all industries and many domains nowadays. I offered the importance of IoT and several use cases for IoT in one of my books titled "A Practical Guide for IoT Solution Architects".

Chapter 3: Big Data Solution Architecture

Definition of Data Architecture

There are various definitions of Data Architecture in the literature. In this book, I'd offer an interpretation which suits the context, content, and purpose of this book.

At the highest level, my definition of Data Architecture is the process of collecting data and manipulating data and data sources from a current state to future state using an architectural framework.

This framework includes describing the structure of the source data, its manipulation process, and the structure of the target data for future use to create business insights from the solution. The architectural term 'description' is the keyword in this definition.

Manipulation refers to the process of moving data, changing data structures, data items, data groups, and data stores. The manipulation process also includes integrating data artefacts to application landscape, communications, interactions, data flow, analysis, locations, and data consumption profiles.

The architectural description refers to describing the life cycle of how data is collected, processed, stored, used and archived. A Big Data solution architect can undertake the accountability of creating the architectural description from current to target state.

Data Layers

As Big Data architects, we use a top-down approach to start the solution description layer by layer.

The first layer for description is the conceptual representing the business entities for data. The second layer is the logical describing the relationship between objects. The third layer is the physical representing the data mechanisms and functionality.

It is essential to highlight that the Big Data architecture is not an end itself, but the value it creates matters. The value is the provision of insights from Big Data and help with decision making for business goals such as increasing profitability, gaining new leads, entry to new markets, or merely reducing the cost for a product or service. Before going further, let's understand what Big Data is.

What is Big Data

One significant fact is that Big Data is ubiquitous. Big data is different from traditional data. The main differences come from characteristics such as volume, velocity, variety, veracity, value and overall complexity of data sets in a data ecosystem.

There are many definitions in the industry and academia however the most succinct yet comprehensive definition which I agree comes from the Gartner: "Big data is high-volume, high-velocity, and high-variety information assets that demand cost-effective, innovative forms of information processing for enhanced insight and decision making". The only missing keyword in this definition is the 'veracity'. I'd also add to this definition that these characteristics are interrelated and interdependent.

Volume refers to the size or amount of data sets in terabytes, petabytes or exabytes. However, there are no specific definitions to determine the threshold for Big Data volumes.

Velocity refers to the speed of producing data. Big Data sources generate high-speed data streams coming from real-time devices such as mobile phones, social media, and IoT sensors, edge gateways and the Cloud.

Variety refers to multiple sources of data. The data sources include structured transactional data, semi-structured such as web site or system logs, and unstructured such as video, audio, animation, pictures.

Veracity means the quality of the data. Since volume and velocity are enormous in Big Data, veracity is very challenging. It is essential to have quality output to make sense of data for business insights.

Veracity is also related to value is the primary purpose of Big Data is to gain business value. The value is created with an innovative and creative approach by all the stakeholders of a Big Data solution.

Overall complexity for Big Data refers to more data attributes and difficulty to extract desired value due to large volume, wide variety, enormous velocity and required veracity for the desired value.

Even though architecturally similar to traditional data, big data requires newer methods and tools to deal with data. The traditional methods and tools are not adequate to process big data. The process refers to capturing a substantial amount of data from multiple sources, storing analysing, searching, transferring, sharing, updating, visualising and governing huge volumes data such as petabytes or even exabytes.

Ironically, the main concern or aim of Big Data is not the amount of data but more advanced analytics techniques to produce value out of these large volumes of data. The advanced analytics in this context refers to approaches such as descriptive, predictive, prescriptive, and diagnostic analytics.

The descriptive analytics deals with situations such as what is happening right now based on incoming data. The predictive analytics refers to what might happen in the future. Prescriptive analytics deals with actions to be taken. Diagnostic analytics ask the question of why something happened. Each analytics type serves difference scenarios and use-cases.

Big Data Lifecycle Management

As Big Data solution architects, we need to understand the lifecycle as we are engaged in all phases of the lifecycle. Our roles and responsibilities may differ in different stages; however, we need to be on top of the life cycle management end to end.

Based on my experience and input obtained from industry publications, from an architectural solutions perspective, a typical Big Data solution, similar to traditional data lifecycle, includes 12 distinct phases in the overall data lifecycle management.

Big Data solution architects are engaged in all phases of the lifecycle, providing different input for each stage. These phases may be implemented under different names in different data solution teams. There is no rigorous universal systematic approach to the Big Data lifecycle as the field is still evolving. For guiding purposes, I propose the following distinct phases:

Phase 1: Foundations

Phase 2: Acquisition

Phase 3: Preparation

Phase 4: Input and Access

Phase 5: Processing

Phase 6: Output and Interpretation

Phase 7: Storage

Phase 8: Integration

Phase 9: Analytics

Phase 10: Consumption

Phase 11: Retention, Backup, and Archival

Phase 12: Destruction

Let's have an overview of each phase with guiding points. These phases can be customised based on the needs of our Big Data solutions. They are not set in stone.

Phase 1: Foundations

In data management process, the foundation phase includes various aspects such as understanding and validating data requirements, solution scope, roles and responsibilities, data infrastructure preparation, technical and non-technical considerations, and understanding data rules in an organisation.

This phase requires a detailed plan facilitated ideally by a data project manager with substantial input from the Big Data solution architect and some data domain specialists.

A Big Data solution project includes details such as plans, funding, commercials, risks, dependencies, and issues, resourcing in a project definition report (PDR). Project Managers author the PDR however, the solution overview in this artefact is covered by the Big Data Architect.

Phase 2: Data Acquisition

Data Acquisition refers to collecting data. Data can be obtained from various sources. These sources can be internal and external to the organisation. Data sources can be structured forms such as transferred from a data warehouse, transaction systems, or semi-structured forms such as Web or system logs or unstructured such as media files consist of videos, audios, or pictures.

Even though data collection is conducted by various specialists and administrators, the Big Data architect has a substantial role in facilitating this phase optimally. Data governance, security, privacy, and quality controls start with the data collection phase hence the Big Data architects take technical and architectural leadership of this phase.

The lead Big Data solution architect needs to document the data collection strategy, requirements, architectural decisions, use cases, and technical specifications in this phase. In large solutions, the lead architect delegates some of these activities to various domain architects and some data specialists.

Phase 3: Data Preparation

In the data preparation phase, the collected data – in raw format- is cleaned or cleansed – these two terms are interchangeably used in different organisations.

In this phase, data is rigorously checked for any inconsistencies, errors, and duplicates. Any redundant, duplicated, incomplete, and incorrect data are removed. The result is to have a clean and useable data set.

The Big Data solution architect facilitates this phase; however, most data cleaning tasks can be performed by data specialists who are trained in data preparation and cleaning techniques.

Phase 4: Data Input and Access

Data input refers to sending data to planned target data repositories or systems. For example, we can send the clean data to determined destinations such as a CRM (Customer Relationship Management) system, a data lake, or a data warehouse. In this phase, data specialists transform the raw data into a useable format.

Data access refers to accessing data using various methods such as using relational databases, flat files, or NoSQL which is more relevant and widely used for the Big Data solutions.

The Big Data solution architect leads this phase; however, usually, a data specialist with the help of database administrators perform the input and access related tasks in this phase.

Phase 5: Data Processing

Data Processing starts with processing the raw form of data. Then, we convert data into a readable format giving it the form and context. After this activity, we can interpret the data by the selected data analytics tools.

We can use standard Big Data processing tools such as Hadoop MapReduce, Impala, Hive, Pig, and Spark SQL. The most common real-time data processing tool is HBase, and near real-time data processing tool is Spark Streaming.

Data processing also includes activities such as data annotation, data integration, data aggregation, and data representation.

Data annotation is labelling the data. Once data is labelled, it can be ready for machine learning.

Data integration aims to combine data exist in different sources and provide the data consumers with a unified view of them.

Data representation refers to the way data is processed, transmitted, and stored. These three essential functions depict the representation of data in the lifecycle.

Data aggregation aims to compile data from databases to combined datasets to be used for data processing.

In the data processing phase, data may change its format based on requirements. Processed data can be used in various data outputs such as in data lakes, for enterprise networks, and connected devices.

We can further analyse the datasets for advanced processing techniques using various tools such as Spark MLib, Spark GraphX, and other machine learning tools.

Data processing require various team members with different skills sets. While the lead solution architect leads the processing phase, most of the tasks are performed by data specialists, data stewards, data engineers, and data scientists. The Big Data architect facilitates the process for this phase.

Phase 6: Data Output and Interpretation

In data output phase, the data is in a format ready for consumption by the business users. We transform data into useable formats such as plain text, graphs, processed images or video files.

The output phase proclaims the data ready for use and sends the data to the next stage for storing. This phase in some organisation is also called data ingestion aiming to import data for immediate use or future use and keep it in a database format.

Data ingestion process can be a real-time or batch format. Some standard Big Data ingestion tools that we can commonly use are Sqoop, Flume, and Spark streaming.

We can interpret the ingested data. The process require analysing ingested data and extract information or meaning out of it to answer the questions related to the solutions developed.

Phase 7: Data Storage

Once we complete the data output phase, we store data in designed and designated storage units. These units are part of the data platform and infrastructure design.

The infrastructure can consist of storage area networks (SAN), network-attached storage (NAS), or direct access storage (DAS) formats. Data and database administrators can manage stored data and allow access to the defined user groups.

Big Data storage includes underlying technologies such as database clusters, relational data storage, or extended data storage, e.g. HDFS and HBASE.

The file formats text, binary, or another type of specialised formats such as Sequence, Avro and Parquet are considered in data storage design phase.

Phase 8: Data Integration

Once the data is stored, in traditional models, it ends the process. However, for Big Data, there may be a need for the integration of stored data for various purposes.

Data integration is a complex and essential domain in Big Data solution process. Big Data architects design use of various data connectors for the integration of Big Data solutions. There may be use cases and requirements for many connectors such as ODBC, JDBC, Kafka, DB2, Amazon S3, Netezza, Teradata, Oracle and many more based on the data sources used in the solution.

Some data models may require integration of data lakes with a data warehouse or data marts. There may also be application integration requirements.

For example, some integration activities may comprise of integrating data with dashboards, tableau, websites, or data visualisations applications. This activity may overlap with the next phase, which is data analytics.

Phase 9: Data Analytics

Integrated data can be useful and productive for data analytics, which is the next phase.

Data analytics is a significant component of Big Data. This phase is critical because this is where business value is gained from Big Data. We can use many tools based on the requirements. The most commonly used tools are Scala, Phyton, and R notebooks.

There can be a team responsible for data analytics led by a chief data scientist. Data architect has a limited role for this phase. Data architects need to ensure the stages of the lifecycle are completed with an architectural rigour.

Phase 10: Data Consumption

Once data analytics takes place, then the data is turned into information ready for consumption by the internal or external users, including customers of the organisation.

Data consumption may have required policies, rules, regulations, principles, and guidelines. The consumption can be based on a service provision process.

Data governance bodies create regulations.

The lead Big Data Architect facilitates the creation of these policies, rules, principles and guidelines using an architectural framework.

Phase 11: Retention, Backup, and Archival

Some critical data may need to be backed up. There are data backup strategies, techniques, methods and tools that the solution architects need to identify, document, and obtain approval.

The Big Data Architect may delegate the design of this phase to an Infrastructure architected assisted by several data, database, storage, and recovery domain specialists.

Some data for regulatory or other business reasons may need to be archived for a defined period of time. Data retention strategy must be documented and approved by the governing body and implemented by the infrastructure architects and storage specialists.

Phase 12: Data Destruction

There may be regulatory requirements to destruct a particular type of data after a certain amount of times. These may change based on the industries and organisations that data belong.

Even though there is a chronological order for the life cycle management, for producing Big Data solutions, some phases may slightly overlap and can be done in parallel.

The life cycle proposed in this book is the only a guideline and can be customised based on the structure of the data solution team, unique data platforms, data solution requirements, use cases, and dynamics of the owner organisation departments or the enterprise.

Now that we had an overview of the phases, let's touch on and understand the Big Data solution components.

Big Data Solution Components

Big data solution architecture begins with an understanding of the Big Data process end to end. Understanding solution components can help us and other stakeholders see the big picture of Big Data process. We can categorise Big Data process under two broad categories. The first one is Data Management, and the second one is Data Analytics.

Data management includes multiple activities as described in the lifecycle, such as data acquisition, extraction, cleansing, annotation, processing, integration, aggregation, and representation.

Data Analytics includes activities such as data modelling, data analysis, data interpretation, and data visualisation.

As Big Data architects, we need to understand the key components in the lifecycle such as data types, principles, platforms, quality specifications, governance, security, privacy analytics, semantics, patterns, data lakes, puddles, swamp, ponds and data warehouse.

These are the fundamentals, and there may be several other components based on the solutions use cases and requirements. In the following sections we have an overview of these fundamental components. Let's start with data types.

Data Types

We can categorise data types as structured, semi-structured, and unstructured. Structured data is traditionally well-managed, relatively more straightforward, and not a big concern of the overall data management process.

However, the challenge is related to semi-structured and more importantly dealing with unstructured data. These two are critical considerations for Big Data solutions. These two data types add real value to obtain the desired information and consume them for business insights.

The primary concern with the semi-structured data is that this type of data does not conform to standards strictly. We can implement semi-structured data with the use of XML (Extensible Markup Language). XML is a textual language for exchanging data on the World Wide Web. XML uses user-defined data tags that make them machine-readable.

Clickstream data is another example of semi-structured data. For example, this type of data provides comprehensive data sets about users' behaviour and their browsing patterns to online shops. This data type is widespread and relevant to Big Data analytics for business insights.

Unstructured data is the concern of text analytics, which aims to extract the required information from textual data. Some textual data examples are blogs, emails, documents, news, and contents in social network sites.

Text analytics include computational linguistics, machine learning, and traditional statistical analysis. Text analytics focus on converting massive volumes of a machine or human-generated text into meaningful structures to create business insights and support decision-making.

We can use various text analytics techniques. For example, information extraction is one of the text analytics techniques which extract structured data from unstructured text.

Text summarisation is another technique which can automatically create a condensed summary of a document or selected groups of documents. This is especially useful for blogs, news, product documents, and scientific papers.

NLP (Natural Language Processing) is another sophisticated text analytics technique interfaced as question and answers in natural language such as Siri in Apple products and Amazon Alexa.

One of the recent growing text analytics technique is sentiment analysis. It aims to analyse people's views about individuals, publications, products or services. This is commonly used for marketing purposes. One example of sentiment analysis is the use of the microblogging site Twitter. We can analyse the twits to obtain positive or negative sentiments for a product or service.

In addition to text analytics, unstructured data is also analysed in human speech. This is referred to as speech analysis or audio analysis in some data management publications. Human speech is commonly used in call centres to improve customer satisfaction and meet specific regulatory requirements.

Another unstructured data analysis is a picture and video content analysis. These are still at infancy, but there is a trend to create new techniques to analyse photos and content of video for information insights.

Due to relatively large size of videos, this is not as easy as text analytics. One of the critical applications of video content analysis is in the security domain commonly used in data generated by the CCTV cameras, automated security, and surveillance systems.

Data Principles

Data management requires established principles. There are country or geography level principles produced by governing bodies. For example, the most popular ones are the GDPR (General Data Protection Regulation) and the CCPA (California Consumer Privacy Act).

In recent years, GDPR became extra popular in the media. GDPR is a regulation in European Union law on data protection and privacy for all individual citizens of the EU and the European Economic Area.

To give you an idea on the data management principles, GDPR offers the following seven principles. These principles sound universal as they are widely repeated in data management publications.

1. Lawfulness, fairness, and transparency

2. Purpose limitation

3. Data minimisation

4. Accuracy

5. Storage limitations

6. Integrity and confidentiality

7. Accountability

We don't need to go into details for each principle here as they can be reviewed from GDPR site. These principles are common sense and straight forward to understand.

These principles cover significant aspects of data management in an organisation. As Big Data architects, we need to consider these principles and apply them to our Big Data solutions.

There may also be principles developed by our organisations' governing bodies in addition to data management policies, processes, procedures and guidelines. Our Big Data solutions need to incorporate these principles.

Data Quality Specifications

Data quality is vital to the end goal of data usage for technical purposes and user consumption purposes. Higher quality in data specifications yields the better-desired results for the solution.

As Big Data architects, we need to consider the critical data quality factors such as data elements being complete, unique, current and conforming. The data quality specifications can be developed using system-generated reports, auditing, and issues raised by users.

Completeness in terms of data quality refers to making sure that necessary elements of data are available at the lifecycle of the data management process. The uniqueness of data refers to having no duplicates of the data elements.

The data currency refers to being up-to-date. Obsolete data is meaningless and useless. Besides, we need to confirm that the data elements are specific to their domains.

Big Data quality can be gauged using relevant data sources, optimised analytical models, and obtaining favourable results translating to data consumer experience and profitability for the enterprise. These results can be tangible or intangible.

Big Data Platform

Every Big Data solution requires a platform. A Big Data platform is consist of several layers. The first layer of the Big Data platform is the shared operational information zone consists of the data types such as data in motion, data at rest, and data in several other forms. It includes legacy data sources, new data sources, master data hubs, reference data hubs, and content repositories.

The second layer is called processing. This substantial layer includes data ingestion, operational information, landing area, analytics zone, archive, real-time analytics, exploration, integrated warehouse, data lakes, data mart zones. This layer needs to have a governance model for metadata catalogue including data security and disaster recovery of systems, storage and hosting and other infrastructure components such as local processing, storage and the Cloud processing and storage.

The third layer is the analytics platform. It consists of real-time analytics, information planning, forecasting, decision making, predictive analytics, data discovery, visualisations, dashboard, and other analytics features as required in the solution.

The fourth layer consists of outputs such as business processes, decision-making schemes, and point of interactions. This platform also needs to be well-governed, and access needs to be provided with established controls both for the data platform professionals such as data scientists, data architects, analytics experts, and business users.

Level of the schema for the data platform is a crucial architectural consideration. We can classify the level of schema under three categories, such as no schema, partially structured schema, and full structured schema. Schema reflects the structure of data and databases. We can think of a schema as a blueprint for data management.

Some examples of no schema are video, audio and picture files; social media feed, partial schema such as email, instant messaging logs, system logs, call centre logs; and high schema can be structured sensor data and relational transaction data.

The data processing levels are the other architectural considerations. The processing levels could be raw data, validated data, transformed data and calculated data.

Other structural classifications of data in data platforms are related the business relevance. We can categorise the business relevance of data as external data, personal data, departmental data, and enterprise data.

Business Vocabulary

Business vocabulary is a critical aspect of data management. We must define the business vocabulary to maintain a shared understanding of big data pertinent to business analytics.

The business vocabulary describes the business content supported by the data models. More importantly, from an architectural perspective, this vocabulary can be a crucial input to the metadata catalogue.

Business vocabulary provides consistent terms to be used by the whole organisation. Business units own the business vocabulary. Usually in many organisations, business users maintain this vocabulary.

Big Data Governance

Data governance is a critical factor for Big Data solutions. The Big Data governance system needs to consider essential factors such as security, privacy, trust, operability, conformance, agility, innovation, and transformation of data. These factors may result in competing actions such as innovation and conformance in two different ends of the spectrum.

It is also vital that at a fundamental level that a data governance infrastructure must be established and evolved for adoption not only in program solution level but also at the enterprise level.

Data governance may take consideration for

different stakeholders in the various platforms. For example, data architects are responsible for developing the governance of big data models; data scientist are accountable for the governance of analytics. Business stakeholders are responsible for the governance of business models for producing business results for the data platforms in concern.

Big Data governance is a broad area and covers data components, scope, requirements handling, strategy, architecture, design, development, analysis, tests, processing, relationships, input, output, business goals, business insights, and all other aspects of data management and analytics process.

Business Thinking for Big Data Architects

Big Data architects not only think in terms of the architectural or technical aspects of the data lifecycle but also think in business and strategic terms.

To start with, the Big Data architects need to understand clear business goals for the organisation to achieve results at a solution, departmental, program, and enterprise levels. We must document the variances of this understanding, request agreement and approval from the business stakeholders.

The next consideration is the relevancy and applicability of data sources to the business goals. We need to ask whether the data sources we plan to use in Big Data solutions are relevant and applicable to the enterprise Big Data goals. We need to identify and point out any irrelevance and duplications. The lead Big Data architect must liaise and closely work with the Enterprise Architects and Business Architects to sort out the data governance concerns from business perspective.

The Big Data solution architects also need to prepare and equipped with customer engagements for their solutions. As Big Data Architects, we must articulate the solution, obtain constant feedback, and make a necessary adjustment during the solution development lifecycle.

Big Data Analytics

Big Data Analytics is a comprehensive business-driven discipline. At a high level, Big Data Analytics aims to make quick business decisions, reduce the cost for a product or service, and test new markets to create new products and services.

Big Data analytics are used by many organisations in various industries. From the industry reports, it is evident that Big Data Analytics solutions are commonly used by several industries such as health care, life sciences, manufacturing, government, retail, education, and several more. The use cases and requirements may differ from one industry to another. Therefore, industry knowledge for Big Data architects is also essential

We need methods and tools to perform Big Data Analytics. There are established methods and many tools available on the market. Most of the methods are proprietary, but some are available via open-source programs.

We need to familiarise with standard Big Data Analytics tools and help with the selection and procurement process. There are many tools but some popular tools commonly used and frequently mentioned in the Big Data Analytics publications are Aqua Data Studio, Azure HDinsight, IBM SPSS Modeler, Skytree, Talend, Splice Machine, Plotly, Lumify, Elasticsearch. In the appendix, as a quick guide, based on on my experience, I provided a list of commercial service providers in these areas.

As we all observe, open-source has progressed well in Big Data Analytics area and produced multiple powerful tools. Some commonly used open-source analytics tools are from the Apache such as Hadoop, Spark, Storm, Cassandra, SAMOA, and other open-source tools such as Neo4j, MongoDB, and R programming environment. We cover the overview of these tools in the technology and tools section of this chapter.

Big Data analytics is a broad and rapidly growing area. We can better understand Big Data Analytics looking at its inherent characteristics as documented in the body of knowledge for Big Data.

We can easily remember these characteristics using nine terms, starting with the letter C. These terms are connection, conversion, cognition, configuration, content, customisation, cloud, cyber, and community. As these terms are self-explanatory, we don't go into details to explain each here.

Big Data analytics use various methods and techniques such as natural language processing, machine learning, data mining, association pattern mining, behavioural analytics, predictive analytics, descriptive analytics, prescriptive analytics, diagnostic analytics. Let's take an overview of these Big Data Analytics types.

Type of Big Data Analytics

As Big Data Architects, even though we don't perform analytics, we still need to understand four major Big Data analytics types to create solutions in these areas.

These four common analytics types are descriptive, predictive, prescriptive, diagnostic. Each type is different in scope and aims to answer different business questions and provide different insights. Let's briefly explain each.

Descriptive Analytics

Descriptive analytics covers the historical aspect of data to understand what happened in the past. It aims to interpret historical data and elicit conclusions from data analysis to gain business insights. Some of the common themes of descriptive analytics are sales growth, new customers, numbers of products sold and many other financial metrics to inform the sales and business executives.

Predictive Analytics

Predictive analytics cover techniques that predict future outcomes based on current and historical data. Predictive analytics look for patterns and capture relationships in data. For example, the use of linear regression techniques in machine learning and neural network to achieve the interdependencies of variables in captured data is commonly used for predictive analytics. It can be used in many disciplines and various business purposes. Predicting customer purchase goals by analysing their shopping behaviour is an everyday use case for Big Data solutions.

Prescriptive Analytics

Prescriptive analytics aims to find the best action for a given situation. This type of analysis looks for ways to determine the best outcome among various choices. Prescriptive analytics can be instrumental in mitigating risks, improve the accuracy of predictions and take benefits of opportunities. It analyses the interactions and potential decisions and provides the best solution.

Diagnostic Analytics

Diagnostic analytics ask the question of why something has happened by examining the data and propose an answer to this fundamental question. It used multiple techniques such as discovery, mining, correlations, contrasting, and so on.

In addition, these four types of analytics, another trending analytics type for Big Data solutions is related to semantic technologies. Semantics Data Analytics is an emerging and complicated process requiring various techniques and tools. Let's discuss this in the next section.

Semantics Data Analytics

As the volume, variety, and velocity of data rising in the enterprise, there is a need to apply semantic technologies to our Big Data solutions in the program level. Using semantic technologies can help our solutions to improve the veracity of data and gain insights from proverbially murky data growing exponentially from multiple sources and in various formats especially in an unstructured format.

Semantic data analytics can be used to create new meanings from unstructured data, particularly in text format. This type of analytics also helps with finding the context and relationships in unstructured data. We can apply semantic analytics to search for the required keywords to make sense of the cluttered text.

The keyword search via semantic analysis can help us automate the data mining techniques. One of the most useful aspects of semantic technology, such as deep learning mechanisms, is provision to annotate the content, context and the real meaning of the data. The graphical representation capability in a semantic model can be beneficial to represent data in a human-understandable way.

The automation of semantic technologies for Big Data requires to integrate semantic knowledge into the data systems and databases. This capability allows the consumers to make easily understandable queries with the necessary meaning behind them as the semantic search is not limited to explicit statements. The traditional search mechanisms are not capable of capturing meaning, context and essential relationships from data sources.

The automation can consider connecting metadata models with semantic technologies to the traditional data warehouse systems in the enterprise. For example, in data science terms, the relationships at various levels such as unary, binary, ternary and 'n-ary' can be described in the semantic taxonomy for automation considerations.

This integration can provide a transformation of data for better quality and more human-understandable formats. This automation process can help our solutions to structure unstructured data to a certain degree. However, the semantic technologies are still evolving; hence, they are no panacea for full-fledged data transformation from unstructured to structured. It worths the architectural considerations for our Big Data solutions.

Evolving Big Data Architecture Patterns

There are two architecture patterns commonly cited in the Big Data publications recently. The first one is the Lambda Architecture, and the second one is the Kappa Architecture pattern. It can be useful to understand both of these evolving patterns.

Lambda is a real-time data processing architecture. As documented in the lambda-architecture.net, resources on this site are attributed to Nathan Marz, Michael Hausenblas, James Kinley, and Christian Prokop. My understanding is that this architecture addresses low-latency reads and updates in a linearly scalable and fault-tolerant way. Lambda architecture consists of three distinct layers, namely a 'batch layer', a 'speed layer', and a 'serving layer'.

The Lambda documentation shows that the batch layer precomputes results using a distributed processing system that can handle enormous quantities of data. The speed layer processes data streams in real-time and without the requirements of fix-ups or completeness. The output from the batch and speed layers are stored in the serving layer. It responds to ad-hoc queries by returning precomputed views or building views from the processed data.

The second commonly cited Big Data enabling architecture pattern is called Kappa. It is documented in http://milinda.pathirage.org/kappa-architecture.com. Based on the information provided on this site, rather than using a relational DB like SQL or a key-value store like Cassandra, the canonical data store in a Kappa Architecture system is an append-only immutable log. From the log, data is streamed through a computational system and fed into auxiliary stores for serving.

The documentation in this site points out that Kappa Architecture is a simplification of Lambda Architecture. A Kappa Architecture system is similar to the Lambda Architecture system with the batch processing system removed. To replace batch processing, data is fed through the streaming system quickly.

These are two sample evolving patterns commonly used by the community. I don't see a value for going into details for these evolving architecture patterns here, however, recommend the Big Data solution architects to review, understand and apply the offering of these architecture patterns.

Decision Management System

Decision management systems are one of the most commonly used applications of Big Data and Analytics. Big Data made decision management systems more powerful and effective for business insights. Big Data, coupled with analytic capabilities, contributed to making more precise decisions for managing high impact risks.

Decision management systems are integral parts of many analytical and AI (Artificial Intelligence) applications. These systems are used almost in all industries and business domains to automate the decision-making process for sophisticated, repetitive, and convoluted information and interdependent data sets.

With enriched Big Data and AI-based or cognitive analytics, the decision management systems provide accelerated solutions to complex business problems when quick decision are required for consumer demands. There is a body of knowledge growing on these systems and associated solutions.

Even though decision management systems are within the responsibility domain Data Scientist and management professionals, it can also be useful for the Big Data and Analytics solution architects to understand these systems as they may be required to be incorporated in some Big Data solutions.

Data Lakes, Ponds, Puddles and Swamps

Big data architecture solutions require the use of the data lake model. Data lakes are fundamental and useful aspects of Big Data lifecycle management. We can define the data lakes in the simplest terms as the dynamically clean and instantly useable data sources made available for specific use purposes.

The primary use case for data lakes for the data consumers is to take advantage of clean data based on self-service without needing technical data professionals.

A data lake can be a single store of transformed enterprise data in the native format. These transformed data stores are usually well reported, visualised and analysed using advanced analytics. A data lake can include structured, semi-structured and unstructured data such as images, videos or sounds.

Data lakes are dynamic stores and can be fed iteratively as further clean data are discovered and transformed from multiple sources in various parts of the enterprise. For example, a data lake can store relational data from enterprise applications and non-relational data from IoT devices, social media, and mobile apps.

There are multiple use cases for data lakes. The most common ones are when real-time data analysis require the data sources coming from various sources. Another use case can be related to the goals of having a complete view of customer data coming from multiple sources. Auditing requirements for corporate compliance and centralisation of data for digital transformation can also be valuable use cases for data lakes.

The business value of data lakes come from being able to perform advanced analytics very quickly for data coming from various real-time sources such as clickstreams, social media, system logs.

Data lakes can have substantial business value. Effective use of data lakes helps the business stakeholders to identify opportunities rapidly, make informed decisions, and act on their decision expeditiously for speed to the market.

Data lakes can be implemented using various data management tools, techniques, and services. There are commercially available tools and services as well as open-source services to establish data lakes. For example, Azure Data Lake, Amazon S3, and Apache Hadoop file system are some data lake implementation enablers to consider for our solutions.

Based on observations from several successful implementations of data lakes, it appears that an excellent choice of platform for data lakes is Apache Hadoop. Hadoop, as an open-source system, is highly scalable, modular, technology agnostic, cost-effective and presents no schema limitations. Many Big Data and Storage solution architects commonly use Hadoop to empower their data platforms.

Designing data lakes require critical consideration of data types. For example, as a principle, if the purpose of data is unknown, it is better to keep data in raw format so that it can be used by data professionals in the future when it is needed.

One of the critical challenges of data lakes is maintaining security as the data comes to the lake in real-time from multiple uncontrolled sources. To address this challenge, a well-governing security architecture with access controls and semantic consistency need to be in place for the data lake. Data lake design is a specialist level activity usually conducted by an experienced data storage architect or data management specialist.

Considering data lakes, we also need to understand the two related data store implementation techniques called data puddles and data ponds. A data puddle and a data pond are relatively smaller purpose-built data platforms usually used by a specific single team mission in an organisation conducted by a marketing group or data scientist.

We can consider data puddles or data ponds as the alternative solution options for data-intensive ETL (Extract, Transform, Load) offloading engagements required by a single team with specific data management requirements.

Unlike data lakes, data puddles and ponds are not data-driven processing allowing informed decisions at enterprise levels. From organisational point of view, we can consider them for departmental or group levels. For example, we can consider data ponds for a data warehouse design in smaller scale.

Probably you have heard about the term data swamps related to data lakes. A data swamp is just the opposite of a data lake. This term refers to an unmanaged data lake that may not be accessible by the intended consumers or may not provide desired value.

From lessons learned in the field of data management and analytics, many unsuccessful implementations of data lakes turned into data swamps. Thus, we need to consider this hard-learned lesson in architecting our Big Data solutions. Now, let's move into the traditional data platforms and touch on a crucial component of data platforms called data warehouse.

Data Warehouse

Unlike data lakes, data warehouse includes optimised databases for analysis of relational data coming from enterprise applications and transactional systems. Data warehouse not only has its well-established data structures and schemas are optimised for queries but also their data is cleaned and transformed. It is essential to highlight that the data in a data warehouse is trusted as a single source of truth.

There are two main data warehouse models, namely, atomic and dimensional. Atomic warehouse model includes a relational database, and a dimensional model may consist of data marts. It is interesting to see the recent trends in Big Data platforms that both atomic and dimensional models also cover the data lake model, such as the implementation of Hadoop.

Besides, a new term was introduced by Garner called 'Logical Data Warehouse'. This term refers to the augmented data warehouse. This understanding makes us integrate new data models to the traditional data warehouse landscape creating a heterogeneously augmented data warehouse.

We also need to consider that the recent trend in the industry is that the data-driven organisations are taking advantage of data lakes by extending their data warehouses. This unique integration provides diverse and advanced data utilisation capabilities creating new models for effective and efficient information management systems. As our bread and butter, let's further delve into architectural considerations for Big Data solutions.

Big Data Architectural Considerations

As the Big Data solution architects, we create custom solutions by understanding the use cases, requirements, the solution scope, business stakeholder aspirations, and customer expectations.

We use our architectural and design skills,

relevant technical knowledge, technology stacks and tools to create these custom solutions. Our custom solutions can be in the form of products or services depending on the goals, objectives, requirements, and the scope of the initiative or the projects.

For Big Data solutions, we need to consider several architectural viewpoints and approaches. From top-down, at the highest level, we need to identify optimal approaches to collecting, storing, processing, analysing, and presenting Big Data based on use cases and the approved requirements.

Big Data solutions require heterogeneous technology stacks and tools to fit the purpose and to create successful outcomes. Let's keep in mind that there is no single technology or tool which can provide all-purpose for developing Big Data solutions in large organisations.

Besides, due to their dependencies and relationships to many components, attributes, and factors in the broader enterprise, Big Data solutions cannot be developed in isolation or silos. We need to consider the entire data ecosystem and break the silos in our thinking and critical architectural factors that may affect the whole enterprise. Of course this gigantic mission is not just Big Data Architects' role and involves many stakeholders however we must show our informed leadership from architectural standpoint.

For Big Data solutions, we must focus on highly-scalable platforms, processes, technology stacks, and management tools. Due to the characteristics of Big Data that we mention in previous sections, scalability is a fundamental non-functional requirement for Big Data solutions. Compromising scalability, even in a small amount for a mission-critical solution, can cause undesirable outcomes, troubled projects, and failed service levels.

Enabling modularity is another fundamental architectural consideration for Big Data solutions. For modularity, we need to ensure the solution modules fit into the big picture. For example, the same data should be able to be used by different projects and technologies rather than creating unnecessary data access silos.

From design point of view, let's touch on some technical points considering data and database attributes. As solution architects, we don't have to be a specialist in data management or database administration; however, we need to be aware of some design points. For example, you may come across the terms ACID and CAP as frequently discussed data governance topics that we need to understand and guide the Big Data solution team.

ACID (Atomicity, Consistency, Isolation, Durability) compliance is an essential guide to guarantee the validity of database transactions and sequence of operations when internal errors or system failures occur. However, ACID compliance may impact scalability.

CAP (Consistency, Availability, and Partition) is another architectural point to consider for distributed database systems. This formula instructs that a trade-off must be made choosing one out of three. The reason is only two out of these three aspects are possible. You may check this from data reference publications to understand the implications in detail for when formulating your solutions.

Big Data solutions require thinking out of the box

and innovative way of doing things. We need to understand the latest technologies and practices for Big Data solutions. For example, there is a trend in the industry for trying new methods of data analysis without binding to traditional EDW (Enterprise Data Warehouse) resources and ETL (Extract Transform Load) processes.

In terms of tools and technology stacks, we can consider mixing open source and commercial systems based on their applicability, meeting our use cases and the requirements. For example, OLTP (Online Transactional Processing) can be designed using commercially available relational databases for structured and open-source Casandra Database supporting semi-structured databases.

We experience that the data sources keep changing, and new sources are being available in our organisations. In addition to our legacy data sources, we need to consider new data sources for our Big Data solutions. As Big Data solution architects, it is one of our primary roles to determine the various type of data sources required in our solutions.

From solution readiness and quality management perspectives, it is vital to determine the timelines of data ingestion. Data ingestion, as a critical aspect of Big Data, is the process of importing, transferring, loading processing and storing data for use.

From a solution design perspective, data ingestion can be synchronous, or an asynchronous batched or rea-time basis. We need to articulate these options with clear reasons based on solution requirements and obtain approvals from our data management subject matter experts and the solution governance body.

Data processing is an essential pint for Big Data solutions. To this end, we need to choose the type of processing to perform whether real-time or batch processing. Our data processing solution may require various approaches such as descriptive, predictive, prescriptive, diagnostic, an ad-hoc. We also need to consider the latency expectation of processing based on the deployment modes that we choose.

Data access is a critical requirement of our Big Data solutions. We need to determine how to access the data based on the use cases and the solution requirements. For example, data access can be random or sequential order.

Besides, we need to consider data access patterns in the solution. Data access patterns are necessary to optimise data access requirements. There are patterns available in data application integration and interface publications. For example, some common patterns are accelerating database resource initialisation, eliminating data access bottlenecks, and hiding obscure database semantics from data users. Leveraging experience of our subject matter experts in embedding these patterns to our solutions can be beneficial.

Database optimisation is an essential architectural practice and can be one of the critical requirements in our Big Data solution initiatives. Data optimisation techniques aim to improve the quality and speed for data access, particularly read and write activities. Some of the critical architectural and design considerations are using appropriate indexes, removing unnecessary indexes and minimising data transfers from client to server.

Sharding is a commonly used implementation technique to consider in our solutions. Sharding can be a necessary technique to consider with caution. Sharding is a kind of database partitioning. It splits an extensive database into smaller units. The primary use case for sharding is to isolate faults or address memory problems for the large data sets which could become a bottleneck. As a guideline, we should consider sharding as a last resort after trying all other optimisation methods. Sharding can have several drawbacks in the implementation and operational phases such as back up problems, indexing issues, and even schema change difficulties.

These are only sample high-level architectural considerations for our Big Data solutions. You can see them as the tip of the iceberg in developing Big Data solutions. Once we start the process and delve into requirements and use cases of our solutions in a particular organisation, we can come across many more considerations based on our industry, project goals, and several other factors which some of them can be beyond our controls.

Therefore, it is essential to follow an established method, leverage the experience of our collaborative solution team, use proven processes, consider well-supported technology stacks and tools to produce successful Big Data architectural solutions.

In terms of technology stack and tools, we need to consider use of open-source. Let's briefly touch on the commonly used and recommended Big Data tool in the open-source space.

Overview of Open Source Big Data Tools

Open source is incredibly important and widespread for information technology hence equally crucial for Big Data and Analytics solutions. Open-source is a type licensing agreement which allows the developers and users to freely use the software, modify it, develop new ways to improve it and integrate to larger projects.

Open-source is a collaborative and innovative approach embraced by many IT organisations, architects, specialists, developers and consumers. Open-source is ideal for start-up companies and those companies with a tight IT budget.

There are growing numbers of open-source tools and technology stacks for Big Data and Analytics. In this section, we cover an overview of some popular and commonly used open-source tools to consider for the Big Data solutions.

As an open-source advocate myself for its compelling technical and business reasons, I highly recommend awareness of these tools for Big Data solution architects. Interestingly, several corporate organisations also support open-source; they further improve them and integrate them into their offerings. Here's a summary of the famous open-source Big Data and Analytics tools.

Hadoop

Apache Hadoop is a powerful computing platform for data storage and processing. Hadoop is so widespread that it is a de-facto standard for Big Data and Analytics solutions.

From an architectural point of view, Hadoop offers several benefits such as scalability with clusters of computers, fault-tolerance, flexibility using simple programming models, and cost-effectiveness due to open-source licencing model.

Hadoop is an ideal environment for handling massive storage pools and extensive data sets using the batch approach in distributed computing environments. Because of these architectural, design, and implementation capabilities, we can use Hadoop for our Big Data and Analytics solutions.

Cassandra

Similar to Hadoop, Apache Cassandra is also widely used for Big Data and Analytics solutions. Cassandra is a semi-structured, NoSQL open-source database management system.

From an architectural and design standpoint, Cassandra is linearly scalable using inexpensive commodity servers, providing high-speed transactions, and fault-tolerance for high availability requirements with clustering implementation.

If our Big Data solution has a specific use case for a transactional system requiring fast response, no single point of failure, and massive scalability with a limited budget, then we may consider Cassandra in our solution.

Kafka

Apache Kafka is an open-source stream processing data platform that allows us to subscribe to commit logs and publish data to any number of systems or real-time applications. Kafka became famous because originally, LinkedIn developed Kafka in Scala and Java platforms and donated it to the open-source community.

From an architectural and design standpoint for the Big Data and Analytics solutions, Kafka can provide a unified, low-latency, fault-tolerant, and high-throughput data platform for effectively managing real-time data feeds. The core architecture of Kafka is based on key terms such as topics and partitions establishing the clusters.

From the solution integration point of view, Kafka is powerful and can provide robust solutions using APIs (Application Programming Interfaces) such as producer, consumer, connectors, and streams. These APIs are essential for integrating Big Data and Analytics solutions.

We can leverage the fault tolerance capability of Kafka for our high availability solution as we can implement it clustering servers with brokers distributed across multiple cluster nodes. In recent years, Big Data solution architects and developers recognised this capability, and they replaced the traditional messaging systems with Kafka.

Flume

Apache Flume became a popular log data management tool in Big Data and Analytics solutions.

The primary function of Flume is to collect, aggregate and move extensive amount of log data in the Big Data and Analytics platforms. Managing a large amount of log data is critical in Big Data solutions.

From an architectural and design standpoint, Flume offers a flexible, fault-tolerant, and extensible data management model. Due to these compelling characteristics, we can consider Flume in our Big Data and Analytics solutions requiring high availability and high performance with reliable failover and recovery mechanisms.

From the developers' perspective, Flume also considered a robust system; hence its implementation is widespread globally in the development communities. Flume was developed using Java language and tested mainly in midrange systems such as Ubuntu, RHEL, SLES and Centos.

NiFi

Apache NiFi is an open-source automation tool designed to automate the flow of data amongst the software components based on flow-based programming model. NiFi is a secure system using TLS (Transport Layer Security) encryption.

This funny name comes from its original development on the Niagara Files software. NiFi originated by Onyara and became part of the open-source community by the National Security Agency (NSA) technology transfer program in 2014. It is currently supported by Cloudera for its commercial and development requirements.

NiFi's architectural components include a Web Server controlling and monitoring the application, Flow Controllers for allocation of resources, Extensions in the form of plugins to integrate with other systems, and a FlowFile repository maintaining the active FlowFiles.

Samza

We can use Apache Samza for our near-real-time stream processing requirements in the Big Data and Analytics solutions. The key functional capability of Samza, unlike batch processing systems, is to provide continues computation and output. This capability makes Samza a compelling tool for Big Data and Analytics solutions.

From an architectural standpoint, Samza provides an asynchronous framework for stream processing. This capability allows building stateful applications that process Big Data coming from multiple sources in near-real-time.

We can consider use of Samza for our high availability and high-performance requirements of our Big Data and Analytics solutions. The primary architectural capabilities of Samza enabling high availability and performance are due to fault-tolerance, stateful processing, and isolation features.

Sqoop

Apache Sqoop has become a popular data transfer tool in Big Data and Analytics platforms. We can use Sqoop as a command-line interface application to transfer data between Apache Hadoop and the relational databases. The name Sqoop originated from the phrase "SQL-to-Hadoop". This short phrase can help us remember its primary purpose.

Sqoop supports incremental loads of a single database table or free form SQL query. We can use Sqoop with Hive (a Datawarehouse application) and HBase (a non-relational distributed database) to populate the database tables.

Through support from commercial companies and collaboration within open-source communities, Sqoop has useful integration features. For example, Informatica provides a Sqoop-based connector, Couchbase software company provides a Hadoop connector, and Microsoft provides a Sqoop-based connector to help transfer data from Microsoft SQL Server databases to Hadoop.

Chukwa

Monitoring data collections is a fundamental task for the Big Data and Analytics platforms hence we need to consider adopting relevant tools and technology stack. One of the popular open-source systems meeting the data platform monitoring functionality is Apache Chukwa.

We can use Chukwa to monitor large distributed data systems in our platform. Chukwa is a powerful monitoring tool because it is built on the MapReduce framework on the HDFS (Hadoop Distributed File System).

From architectural and design perspectives of our data platforms, we can rely on Chukwa's scalability and resilience inherited by Hadoop's high availability features.

Storm

Our Big Data and Analytics platform require streaming engines. One of the popular tools in addition to Spark Streaming and Flink is the Apache Storm. The Storm can be an essential tool in our data platform because it also enables real-time data processing.

The Storm framework is made up of two types of nodes: master nodes and worker nodes. Master node's functionality is to execute the Nimbus daemon assigning tasks to nodes in the framework and monitoring their performance.

The Storm architecture offers two critical components called spouts and bolts to define data sources in the data platform. The Storm applications can be designed using a directed acyclic graph (DAG) consist of spouts and bolts. These two components (spouts and bolts) are integrated to allow both batch and distributed processing of streaming data. From usability perspective, the Storm topology helps the application form the graph vertices.

Spark

To understand critical function of Spark, we need consider the MapReduce requirements. MapReduce process is designed to receive input from a storage disk, map the function representing the data, then reduce the results, and stores reduced maps on the disk. The reason we provided this additional information is that The Apache Spark was developed to address some limitations of MapReduce cluster computing.

In recent years, Apache Spark is used as a general-purpose cluster computing framework for data platforms, especially for distributed environments. As a robust suite of products, Spark comes with various distinct components such as Spark Core, Spark SQL, Spark Streaming and Spark GraphX.

From an architectural and design standpoint, Spark represents a resilient distributed dataset (RDD) and provides two key benefits: fault tolerance and data parallelism. Spark's Dataframe API is implemented as an abstraction layer on of this resilient distributed dataset framework.

Hive

Data query, reporting, and analysis are critical functions for Big Data solutions. Many data platforms use a data warehouse system as central data repository to create business intelligence in an organisation. Data warehousing is where Apache Hive plays a critical role.

Apache Hive is a popular data warehouse application built on Hadoop technology stack. The Hive offers a data query language which is called HiveQL, and it supports the analysis of large datasets stored in the HDFS (Hadoop Distributed File System) which can efficiently run on commodity servers. From a cost management perspective, the Hive can be a beneficial tool to include in our Big Data and Analytics solutions.

One of the vital functions of the Hive is to help portability of SQL based applications to Hadoop platform. Facebook developed the Hive initially and further developed by Netflix. In recent years, it became part of critical web services such as Amazon Web Services and Elastic MapReduce.

HBase

We mentioned HDFS (Hadoop Distributed File System) numerous times while discussing the open-source Big Data and Analytics tools. This time we mention it to clarify the role of HBase in the data platform.

Apache HBase is a non-relational distributed database, and it runs on top of the HDFS. It provides Bigtable-like capabilities for Hadoop. HBase is a fault-tolerant system.

To understand one of the significant functions of the HBase we need to know the differences between dense and sparse Data. These are two common terms in IoT data solutions. Dense data represents the values change constantly, and sparse data represents the values change rarely. The HBase offers a robust mechanism to store large quantities of sparse data. HBase resembles Google's BigTable, in fact, it was modelled considering the features of the BigTable. Hence, the IIBase provides similar capabilities of the BigTable for the Hadoop platform.

MongoDB and RocksDB

So far we covered some of the critical Apache suits of products for Big Data. However, these two open-source databases (MongoDB and RocksDB) are prevalent for the Big Data solutions, especially for high performance and high availability requirements.

MongoDB is a high performance, fault-tolerant,

scalable, cross-platform, and NoSQL database. MongoDB deals with unstructured data. This database was developed by MongoDB Inc and is licensed under the SSPL (Server-Side Public License). SSPL is a kind of open source product hence we cover it in this section.

RocksDB offers fast and low-latency storage. RocksDB is part of the MyRock software suite which is also an open-source product. MyRock software was developed by Facebook. The purpose was to use MySQL features with the RocksDB.

In this section, we cover only some widespread open-source tools for Big Data and Analytics solutions. Covering all open-source tools can go beyond the scope and limits of this book. Therefore, it is essential to know that there are many more rapidly developing open-source software tools which can be used for various functions of Big Data life cycle management. My recommendation is to review the tools based on your unique Big Data solution requirements and use cases.

Commercial Big Data and Analytics Tools

Due to importance and growing demands of Big Data and Analytics solutions globally, there are many commercially available tools and technology stacks on the market. Some of these tools offer similar functionality with the open-sources, some additional functionality, and some integrate with open-source tools to optimise and further improve the functions.

Since the numbers of these tools are quite large, it is not possible to include them in this condense book. To keep the size of the book at a reasonable number, I create awareness for existence of these tools and provide the list in the Appendix for your information.

My recommendation is to review these tools compared to the popular open-source tools that we covered in previous section and introduce them to your unique Big Data and Analytics platform. To reiterate, from architectural point of view, your solution requirements, use cases, and commercial policies of your organisation can provide guidelines to choose appropriate technology stacks and tools.

Chapter Summary and Key Points

Data Architecture is the process of manipulating data and data sources from a current state to future state using an architectural framework.

A Big Data architect uses a top-down approach to start the solution description.

The key characteristics of Big Data are volume, velocity, variety, veracity, value.

Even though architecturally similar to traditional data, big data requires newer methods and tools to deal with data.

The descriptive analytics deals with situations such as what is happening right now based on incoming data.

The predictive analytics refers to what might happen in the future.

Prescriptive analytics deals with actions to be taken.

Diagnostic analytics ask the question of why something happened.

Big Data has nine phases, including Foundations, Acquisition, Preparation, Input, Processing, Output and Interpretation, Storage, Integration, Analytics, Consumption, Retention, Backup, and Archival, and Destruction.

Data types can be categories as structured, semi-structured and unstructured.

One of the recent growing text analytics technique is sentiment analysis.

GDPR principles are lawfulness, fairness, transparency, purpose limitation, data minimization, accuracy, storage limitations, integrity, confidentiality, and accountability.

Key data quality factors are being complete, unique, current and conforming.

The Big Data governance system needs to consider critical factors such as security, privacy, trust, operability, conformance, agility, innovation and transformation of data.

Big Data architects not only think in terms of the architectural or technical aspects of the data lifecycle but also think in business and strategic terms.

Big Data Analytics is a business-driven discipline. At a high level, it aims to make quick business decisions, reduce the cost for a product or service, and test new market to create new products and services.

Characteristics of Big Data Analytics include the terms connection, conversion, cognition, configuration, content, customisation, cloud, cyber, and community.

Semantic data analysis can be used to create new meanings from unstructured data, especially in text format.

Some popular Big Data architecture patterns are called the Lambda and the Kappa Architecture patterns.

Data lakes in the simplest terms can be defined as the dynamically clean and instantly useable data sources made available for specific purposes.

Use of data lakes helps the business stakeholders to identify opportunities quickly, make informed decisions, and act on their decision rapidly for speed to the market.

Data swamps refer to an unmanaged data lake that may not be accessible by the intended consumers or may not provide desired value.

Data puddle is a tiny purpose-build data platform usually used by a specific single team mission.

Data ponds can resemble a data warehouse designed for Big Data processing.

Data warehouses include optimised databases for analysis of relational data coming from enterprise applications and transactional systems.

Big Data solutions require heterogeneous technology and tools to fit the purpose. There is no single technology or tool which can provide all-purpose for developing Big Data solutions.

Scalability is critical for Big Data solutions.

ACID (Atomicity, Consistency, Isolation, Durability) compliance is a valuable guide to guarantee the validity of database transactions and sequence of operations.

CAP (Consistency, Availability, and Partition) is an architectural point to consider for distributed database systems. This theorem advises that we need to trade-off one out of three as only can have two out of these three aspects.

We should consider mixing open source and commercial systems based on their applicability and meeting our solution requirements.

Data ingestion is the process of importing, transferring, loading processing and storing data for use.

Sharding can be a necessary technique to consider with caution.

Some standard Big Data open source tools are Apache Hadoop, Cassandra, Kafka, Flume, NiFi, Samza, Sqoop, Chukwa, Storm, and MongoDB.

We may also consider commercially available Big Data and Analytics tools standalone or integrated with open-source technology stacks and tools.

Chapter 4: Cloud for Big Data

Purpose of This Chapter

I dedicate this chapter to Cloud Computing as a critical enabler of Big Data and Analytics solutions. You may think who didn't hear about Cloud computing and who don't know its importance. You are right. My purpose is not to repeat the content of myriad of Cloud publications and books on the market. However, I want to create necessary awareness for its importance and use for creating robust Big Data and Analytics solutions.

Our organisations, business ventures, and overall society rapidly accepted the importance of Cloud Computing and leveraged many benefits of it globally. This technology is rapidly growing and shaking the whole IT landscape. It became ubiquitous.

In this section, we focus on Cloud Computing architecture, service model, and the value proposition for the Big Data and Analytics solutions to supplement the core theme of this book which is the Big Data. Let's start with the Cloud Service Model in our context.

Cloud Service Model

The most desirable attributes of Cloud Computing for Big Data and Analytics solutions are elasticity and scalability. These two terms are critical architectural factors for Big Data and Analytics solutions.

The Cloud service model can expand or reduce computer resources based on service requirements of our solutions. For example, Cloud can provide the maximum amount of resources when we need a large amount of computing power or storage capacity for a specific Big Data and Analytics workload at a particular timeframe.

Then we can release these previously allocated resources after completing the specific mission of our workloads. This elasticity and scalability provide tremendous value position for our business as far as the Big Data and Analytics solutions are concerned.

Concerning scalability and elasticity, from financial perspective, the 'pay per use' or 'pay as you go' model is another essential characteristic that Cloud services offerings provide. In other words, we can consume the compute, storage, and network resources based on the required usage amount. Our usage could be a short — mid, or long-term basis. For example, depending on our needs, we can pay based on computing power, storage amount, or network bandwidth that we use.

Related to 'pay per use', using 'on-demand' is another characteristic of the Cloud services model. We can use when we demand the required services without upfront payment or dedicated investment for the IT resources in the service provider's organisation. However, there are different cost models by different public Cloud service providers.

The recent commercial trend for using virtual machines in publicly available Cloud services are based on three types of instances such as on-demand instance, reserved instance and spot instance. In on-demand instance, there is no long term commitment. Reserved instance is a relatively longer-term with a substantial discount compared to on-demand usage. The spot instance, the price is agreed based on bidding.

Another architectural characteristic that we are interested in our Big Data and Analytics solutions is the resiliency. Resiliency means that system failures such as servers or storage units can be automatically isolated with predefined instructions, and workloads are migrated to redundant virtual units without disrupting the service levels or consumer usage. Cloud's resilience attribute removes many of our supportability concerns in our solution requirements.

From an architectural point of view, based on our solution requirements, Cloud resources can be virtual or physical. The multitenancy characteristic of the Cloud service model creates this flexibility. For example, a Cloud service provider can host multiple user workloads in the same infrastructure without adversely affecting the privacy and security of the consumers. If there are high-security requirements such as sensitive governmental services or trade secrets, isolation can be physical.

For our Big Data and Analytics solutions, we need to carefully consider constraints and limitations which can affect the use of virtual services in multi-tenancy mode. This consideration may require an architectural or commercial decision.

Flexible workload movement is another crucial attribute of Cloud service model. There may be times we require to run our workloads in a different time zone. In this case, our workloads can easily be moved to a data centre in another state or country. We can consider this option for several reasons such as reducing cost, providing a better service for a focus group in a different location or even regulatory requirements.

After reviewing these useful attributes of the Cloud services for our Big Data and Analytics solutions, now let's touch on deployment models which can also provide additional architectural benefits in the solution development lifecycle.

Cloud Deployment Models for Big Data

This section provides an overview in a specific context and not intended to be a general introduction. Therefore, it is condensed. Our focus in this section is on the architectural considerations of Cloud Computing and their implications for Big Data, Analytics and IoT solutions.

One key piece of information we need to keep in mind that Cloud services are based on three major service models. IaaS (Infrastructure as a Service), PaaS (Platform as a Service) and SaaS (Software as a Service). There are also several other service types, but instead of using their names, we collectively call them XaaS. This acronym covers any computing service that can be delivered via the internet and consumed pay as you go model without upfront purchase for their infrastructure or required licenses.

As Big Data architects, most likely, we use PaaS with Big Data platform services enabled. However, there is also the possibility that we can use SaaS, to use specific application packages provided through the Cloud services.

However, for Big Data purposes, there is a trend to provide Big Data services as a unique offering. This unique offering is called Big Data as a Service (BDaaS).

We cover BDaaS in the next section.

Another fundamental point that we need to consider is the deployment models for Cloud. There are four types of deployment models for Cloud-based services. They are public, private, hybrid, and community.

Public Cloud is the most commonly used by small and medium-sized businesses, start-up companies and individuals. Public Cloud services are provided by large service providers such as Amazon, Google, Microsoft, SalesForce, Rackspace, and many more. It is a shared infrastructure and platform for consumers. Most likely, we can use public cloud model for our non-sensitive Big Data and Analytics solutions.

Private Cloud is usually established privately by large organisations using Cloud technologies for overall IT management usually hosted on-premises or rented data centres. The primary purpose of a private Cloud is security and regulatory compliance. There may be some requirements to run our Big Data, Analytics and IoT solutions in the private cloud. Therefore, we need to understand the implications of this model from an architectural and commercial perspective.

Hybrid Cloud is a combination of private and public offerings. For example, an organisation can use private Cloud for their particular workload which requires security and regulatory compliance, and they can also subscribe to a public Cloud for their other generic workloads such as a proof of concept or development and test environments. The hybrid model is another option for our Big Data and Analytics solutions which can be determined based on the requirements.

There is also a Community Cloud deployment model which is usually shared by some organisations for collaboration and other business cooperation purposes. It is the connection of private Cloud access to each other's allocated partition of the Cloud services. These commonly accessed Cloud services can be hosted internally or externally. The Community Cloud deployment model is another option for some workloads, especially for non-profit organisations.

As Big Data solution architects, we need to consider these deployment models and choose the most appropriate model for our solution based on our requirements. Just to recap, for example, if our Big Data solution is very sensitive and cannot pass other geographies, then we need to consider a private Cloud service.

BDaaS (Big Data as a Service)

BDaaS (Big Data as a Service) is a new and evolving Cloud-based service designed for Big Data and Analytics solutions. It is a kind of outsourcing model for Big Data projects. The service has different facets. The most common type of BDaaS is a supply of data management, analysis, and analytical tools performing the actual analysis and providing required visualisation reports in various formats. Besides, some DBaaS service providers can also offer additional services such as advisory and consulting services to complement their consumption-based services.

BDaaS is an excellent opportunity for small business or start-ups, and even large organisations with a limited budget for Big Data and Analytics solutions. It can increase competitiveness, innovation, and revenues for these type of organisational needs.

Architecturally, the BDaaS offering is based on SOA (Service Oriented Architecture) combined with virtualised Big Data storage, scalable, and event-driven processing and analytics tools provided Cloud service and consumption model.

There are different deployment models for BDaaS. Some service providers provide core, performance-based, feature-based, and integrated BDaaS services. The terms and conditions may be different for each service provider. The critical consideration for the Big Data and Analytics solutions perspective is to be aware of the requirements and which service model fits into the requirements of the solution in the most cost-effective way.

The architectural solution benefits of BDaaS are rapid deployment, capacity and scalability on-demand, and established QoS (Quality of Services) for network speed and SLAs (Service Level Agreements). The significant business benefits can be the agility and cost-effectiveness with guaranteed service levels without an upfront investment of funds on massive internal IT costs.

BDaaS is a relatively new service offering, and it is proliferating. We can find many Cloud service organisations providing Big Data and Analytics based on self-service in their Big Data service platforms. Some well known BDaaS providers are Amazon Web Services, Google Cloud Dataproc, Salesforce Wave Analytics, IBM BigInsights on Cloud, Microsoft Azure HDInsight, and Qubole Data Service.

Business Benefits of the Cloud for Big Data

There are many business benefits and compelling use cases of Cloud Computing for Big Data and Analytics solutions and particularly for Big Data processing, storage, and reports.

Speed to market for Big Data solutions is crucial for competitive advantage in business. The cloud service model is ideal to meet this critical business challenge and the requirements.

Big Data can be sent to Cloud-based data lakes with breakneck speed. The analytics engines in the Cloud infrastructure can be made in the required power thanks to the elasticity and scalability of the Cloud services model as mentioned in previous sections. Increasing resources in traditional infrastructure model, as opposed to Cloud services, can be slower and more costly.

Cost is an inevitable business factor for enterprises. Cloud computing pay as you go and on-demand characteristics can make the solutions more economically viable by reducing total cost of ownership. Use of Cloud services based on consumption is sharing financial risk with an outsourcing organisation.

In terms of cost, also the Cloud service model can help reduce management overhead of the infrastructure resources. Infrastructure support costs can be very high. For example, supporting traditional infrastructure systems requires many professionals supporting the operations, procurement of the hardware, software and other components for different purposes can increase the cost substantially for an organisation. The cost incurred by those employees and upfront hardware and software costs is reduced by using Cloud services for complex Big Data and Analytics solutions.

By using Cloud service model, creating a proof of concept or pilots for Big Data and Analytics solutions can be performed in much shorter times without upfront investment for required hardware, software, and other infrastructure components. This lowered cost is especially more important for smaller and start-up companies with limited IT budget. Effective cost management is a desirable proposition for entrepreneurs and start-up companies.

Using Cloud-based Big Data services, the analytics processes can be completed in faster speed with reliable service levels providing speed to market for the business. This can enable new revenue streams for the data in motion, which could be much more difficult in traditional settings in relatively shorter timeframes with established SLAs.

For the complex Big Data solutions, the use of Cloud services can provide a cultural shift. This positive cultural shift can yield more productivity for the solution teams. The teams can collaborate better and be more innovative as they don't have to worry about a myriad of in-house infrastructure issues.

Access to Cloud services can be tailored based on the user's profiles and can be taken from their desks or any location they may prefer working from using any device they may need. Through the use of proof of concepts and easy to use sandbox environments in Cloud services, they can be more experiential, innovative and uplifting for improving their solutions.

Cloud Quality and Adoption Considerations

From an architectural perspective, the quality of Cloud services for Big Data solutions have several characteristics. As Big Data solution architect aiming to use Cloud services for our solutions, we need to consider several fundamental architectural points. We cannot just subscribe to a public Cloud service or only assume a private Cloud environment without performing due diligence.

We can develop a checklist for fundamental and desirable requirements. The following are some essential points to take into consideration. Let's beware that this is not an exhaustive list. It covers a few key points at a high level. However, it can give you an idea of crucial points to consider.

We can start reviewing the Cloud governance structure. Governance is critical for Big Data and Analytics solutions. The solution needs to meet regulatory compliance requirements. For example, privacy is one of the key regulatory considerations as far as Big Data is concerned.

By using the expertise of security analysts or specialists, we need to look into all aspects of security, including authentication, identity management, authorisation, encryption, and many other security aspects. Security is a fundamental systemic matter for Cloud solutions and services. One way of looking at it is whether you can trust the security of this specific Cloud solution or services to host your Big Data project.

Business continuity and disaster recovery must be implemented, tested and validated both in public and private Cloud services. We need to check whether security and privacy are independently audited for the services which we plan to consume.

All non-functional requirements such as performance, availability, scalability, capacity, interoperability, and many more need to be analysed, tracked and validated. We need to review service level agreements for these non-functional requirements; for example, how much uptime is guaranteed and what kind of performance levels are warranted, and more importantly cost of the update and performance as they can be prohibitive.

Cloud processes and services must be clearly articulated in relevant documents accessible to the Big Data and Analytics solution team and relevant data consumers of these solutions. The usability of these documents is essential too.

Network connections and all other connectivity requirements must be verified and validated with the Cloud service providers. Fundamentally, no network, no Cloud! We may check what carriers are being used, what networking technology stack and tools are used in the Cloud infrastructure. Big Data and Analytics processes are entirely dependent on the network when the Cloud services are used for the solutions.

Applications, middleware components, and other tools in the Cloud platform must be ready for use. From a Big Data and Analytics solution perspective, we need to determine whether these applications, middleware tools, and other tools fit the purpose of our solutions.

In addition, these tools may require customisation, tuning and unique configurations. As Big Data solution architects, it is our responsibility to determine these requirements and ensure they are covered in the solution supportability documentation.

System integration facilities, especially APIs also need to be made available in the Cloud hosting services. We need to check that if required, whether we can integrate our solutions based on provided integration infrastructure, APIs, and other tools.

More importantly, as relevant to Big Data, the data management services and analytics tools need to be ready for use. Our subject matter experts need to verify the availability of these tools in the determined service agreement. As a good practice, we can start to test the Cloud services with a small proof of concept to ensure it meets our Big Data solution requirements.

To start the Cloud adoption process for our Big Data and Analytics solutions, we need to create a comprehensive Cloud transition plan. This plan must cover every aspect of the adoption with multiple stakeholders in the organisation. It covers not only technical and architectural matters but also business, project, commercial, and financial matters. It is the solution architect's responsibility to ensure that the Cloud hosting environment is optimal to serve the Big Data solution.

To this end, we need to understand the quality of the services provided for the Cloud adoption and review the service level agreements to match our operational goals to host our Big Data and Analytics solutions.

An architectural requirements traceability and mapping the solution requirements with the provided service level can be a good practice to ensure the operability and serviceability of our Big Data solution.

After these rigorous architectural concerns, let's take a quick look at two vital technical points which can affect our Big Data solutions hosted in a Cloud service model. They are the use of data lakes and APIs in the Cloud environment.

Cloud for Data Lakes

Due to performance, availability, and scalability characteristics of Cloud, it can be instrumental in deploying data lakes in the private Cloud infrastructure or use service-based data lakes in public Cloud offerings. Use of data lakes in Cloud service model can empower diverse sets of analytic engines for Big Data processing.

Creating or using data lakes in the Cloud environments is not only economical but also more accessible, more secure, more reliable, and agile for faster deployments. Data lakes must be trusted, consistent and available for self-service by all authorised consumers. We need to ensure that the service levels cover these critical attributes.

We also touch the data lakes in the Big Data chapter in this book. You can find more information on the importance of using data lakes and how they are implemented for Big Data management and analytics solutions.

APIs for IoT, Cloud and Big Data

APIs (Application Programming Interfaces) are part of the IoT, Cloud and Big Data ecosystem to allow secure connections to the consumers, business communication channels, and other IoT, Cloud and Big Data applications. APIs are used to integrate devices, applications, data, analytics, and Cloud systems efficiently and effectively.

Further, APIs can contribute to the performance, availability, and security goals for integration of these services. For example, IoT devices which use standard APIs can obtain necessary security updates immediately through the Cloud as soon as any security breach happens in the infrastructure. This IoT and Cloud computing integrated approach is a critical enabler of security and privacy without impacting cost, performance or availability.

APIs also help the production of solutions in an agile and cost-effective manner. APIs are and can be compelling components of the IoT, Cloud and Big Data ecosystem using an integrated design.

Big Data technologies and tools have their APIs written in conventional languages such as Java. These APIs help Big Data professionals to access Big Data systems from their tools or applications. Queries can be made via APIs quickly and effectively.

The most useful web services API is called REST shorten from Restful. It is flexible, simple and compatible with various tools and technologies on the web. REST APIs are ideal for accessing different kinds of data sources and interfaces in different tools and platforms.

Chapter Summary and Key Points

The cloud service model can expand or reduce computer

resources based on service requirements.

The Cloud services are provided on-demand and consumption-based pay as you go model.

Cloud workloads can easily be moved from one location to another. This is an ideal use case for Big Data.

Cloud services are based on three major service models. IaaS (Infrastructure as a Service), PaaS (Platform as a Service) and SaaS (Software as a Service).

Public Cloud is the most commonly used by small and medium-sized businesses, start-up companies and individuals.

The primary purpose of a private Cloud is security and regulatory compliance.

Hybrid Cloud is a combination of private and public.

BDaaS (Big Data as a Service) is a new Cloud-based service for Big Data solutions.

Speed to market for Big Data solutions is crucial for competitive advantage in business. The cloud service model is ideal to meet this critical business challenge and requirement.

Cloud computing pay as you go and on-demand characteristics can make the solutions more economically viable by reducing total cost of ownership.

Using Cloud can speed up proof of concepts for testing new business ideas. It is ideal for entrepreneurs with a limited budget.

Network availability, quality and speed are essential factors for Cloud services.

Creating data lakes in Cloud is not only economical but

also more accessible, more secure, more reliable and agile for faster deployments.

APIs (Application Programming Interfaces) are part of the IoT, Cloud and Big Data ecosystem to allow secure connections to the consumers, channels and other IoT, Cloud and Big Data applications.

The most useful web services API is called Rest shorten from Restful.

Chapter 5: IoT for Big Data

Purpose of this Chapter

The purpose of this chapter is to provide an overview of the IoT solutions in relations to the Big Data and Analytics solutions. We also cover the Cloud computing for empowering IoT based Big Data and Analytics solutions.

IoT Value Propositions

The main benefit and value proposition of IoT comes from collecting an enormous amount of data from various means and devices and then building services based on analyses of these massive amounts of data sets. Developing new services from such a collection of data would result in a substantial outcome with multiple implications.

IoT helps us predict the future; hence, the more data provided by the IoT systems, the better the analyses and outcomes can be. These data-rich analyses help us predict the future better and intervene before any potential damage occurs.

As IoT synthesises data via cognitive analytics, IoT solutions can help us gain better insights from structured, semi-structured, unstructured, dynamic or static data by integrating with cognitive systems. Like humans, a cognitive system undertakes the duties of learning, understanding, planning, problem-solving, deciding, analysing, synthesising, and assessing.

IoT solutions can be consumed in many facets of our lives to control our economies. These solutions can be used at home or in our workplaces for various reasons. IoT systems are expected to get smarter. These progressive, smart devices can predict what we need and want.

These devices can even construct bridges between generations. For example, they can help us create a memory repository, which can then be passed on to the next generations to preserve knowledge and shed light on their ancestral heritage.

As an extended electronic ecosystem, IoT solutions can help to eliminate cumbersome technology. For example, undesirable noise, screens, and hardware clutter can shade gradually, and we only deal with the active service providers around us. In other words, technology can be supportive, rather than intrusive.

Several applications are used for IoT. Some typical applications of IoT solutions are home entertainment, home automation and control such as smart lighting, industrial control, robotics, medical data collection, workplace safety, and security, embedded sensing in buildings, remote control, traffic control and most recently self-driving cars.

Implications of Massive IoT Data

IoT devices generate massive amounts of data on an ongoing basis. These data sets go to the full data management lifecycle; for example, storing, analysing, re-building, and archiving.

From architectural perspective, the amount of data

produced by IoT devices require careful performance, capacity, scalability, availability, and monitoring measures.

We need to simulate the actual workload models based on the functional and non-functional requirements. We also need to consider historical data and future growth as part of the requirements analysis for performance.

Data collection via IoT sensors needs to be planned carefully. First, we need to determine the type of physical signals to measure. Then, we need to identify the number of sensors to be used, and the speed of signals for these sensors in our Big Data acquisition plan.

In addition to the challenges of massive data, application usage patterns are also an essential factor for performance. In particular, the processors and memory of the servers hosting the IoT applications need to be considered carefully using benchmarks.

Using benchmarks for application, data, and infrastructure, we need to create an exclusive IoT performance model and a set of test strategies. The IoT performance model mandates more data storage capacity, faster processes, more memory, and faster network infrastructure.

While in the traditional performance models, we mainly consider user simulations, in the IoT Performance models, we also consider the simulation of devices, sensors, actuators, and gateways.

From a data management perspective, it is paramount to be aware of data frequency shared amongst devices. This means that not only the amount of data produced and processed but also accessed and shared frequently across multiple entities of the IoT ecosystem.

The monitoring of these devices also creates a tremendous amount of data. If we always add the alerts and other system management functions to keep these devices well-performing and available, we need to have a comprehensive performance model, including the system and service management of the complex IoT ecosystem.

IoT Cloud

We all know the recent growing trends for Cloud Computing. Cloud marked a paradigm shift to Information Technology and Computing field. IoT Cloud is a critical player in the overall data ecosystem. The central role the Cloud plays in IoT is to facilitate the data integration of the solution components.

IoT solutions are mainly used to provide real-time information to consumers. The data required to generate real-time data can be massive in scale. The Cloud, along with computing power, storage, network, analytics, metering, and billing components, can make this information available for the consumers.

The integration of Cloud to IoT can create new revenue streams from our Big Data. Integrating the Cloud with the IoT can create new business models enriched by real-time analytics and directly-consumed information anywhere at the same time. In other words, without the Cloud, the IoT can hardly add any value due to its real-time data and information-rich nature.

The addition of the Cloud to the IoT can also contribute to improved security, availability, and performance of the IoT based Big Data and Analytics solutions. Cloud providers have rigorous security, availability and performance metrics established based on a service consumption model. In particular, IoT-enabled Cloud systems seem to pose additional security measures.

When integrated with Edge computing in the IoT ecosystem, Cloud computing can add better value to the IoT based Big Data and Analytics solutions. The main reason for this is that Edge computing can do the filtering for the Cloud to focus on the usable data.

Therefore, it is essential for the IoT and Big Data solution architects to understand the Cloud Computing service models and how they can be integrated into the IoT and Big Data solutions. Being aware of the capabilities of Cloud technology stacks and tools can be beneficial in creating large-scale commercial IoT, Big Data and Analytics solutions.

IoT and Big Data Analytics Computation in Cloud

IoT solutions need computers to perform Big Data and Analytics solutions for business intelligence. Such resource-hungry workloads are hosted by Cloud platforms, such as analytics applications for which computation performance is essential. We also need to consider storage capacity, scalability and performance. For analytics storage, we need to make an architectural decision as to whether local storage or cloud-based storage could effectively fit our solution. This architectural decision is necessary to address both cost and performance concerns.

IoT Analytics can also be provided as a consumption-based service. For example, AWS IoT Analytics is a fully-managed IoT analytics service that collects, pre-processes, enriches, stores and analyses IoT based Big Data. AWS customers can also bring their custom analytics packaged in a container to execute AWS IoT Analytics.

We use analytics to make sense of Big Data, such as key performance indicators in the visualisation application in a dashboard. These dashboards can include risk management views, errors, bottlenecks, and view things in real-time.

Data Lakes for IoT

IoT introduces new ways to collect data from various real-time data sources coming from the sensors of connected devices such as smart products, vehicles and other moving devices which ends up in Big Data forms. Using a data lake for IoT generated Big Data makes it easier to store and perform analytics for IoT data.

The speed of using clean data (aggregated in a single place) for analytics can help discover ways to reduce operational costs and increase the quality of ingested data.

As more products, assets, vehicles and other "things" are instrumented and data ingested, it's essential that IoT data sets be aggregated in a single place, where they can be easily analysed and correlated with other relevant data sets using Big Data processing capabilities. Doing so is critical to generating the gain most leverage and insights from IoT based Big Data.

IoT Architectural Challenges

There are several challenges related to IoT solutions. The challenges are architectural, technical, and non-technical. The most common architectural challenges for IoT are mobility, scalability, capacity, extendibility, interoperability, network bottlenecks, and connectivity.

Mobility is a common IoT Architecture Non-Functional aspect. IoT devices need to move a lot and change their IP address and networks frequently based on their locations. For example, the routing protocols, such as RPL, must reconstruct the DODAG (Destination Oriented, Directed Acyclic Graph) each time a node goes off the network or joins the network, which adds substantial overhead to the system. These minute technical details from outside, which concern mobility, may have a severe impact on solution performance, availability, security, and cost.

IoT Solutions require overall scalability and capacity plans. IoT applications integrate with and serve multiple devices in the enterprise data ecosystem. Managing the distribution of devices across networks and the application landscape is a complicated task. There is a need for a dynamic increase or decrease in capacity, coupled with vertical and horizontal scalability and extendibility of the solutions. IoT applications need to be tolerant of new services and devices joining the network at a fast speed. Addressing this challenge requires dynamic scalability and enormous extendibility.

Interoperability means that heterogeneous devices, solution components, elements, and protocols need to be able to work with each other harmoniously. Maintaining the interoperability in an IoT ecosystem is another challenge owing to the wealth of platforms, solution components, devices and protocols used in IoT ecosystems.

Network bottlenecks adversely affect availability, performance and the cost of products or services in productions, making the service level agreements challenging to meet. Apart from latency related to the distance, several other factors are causing the network bottlenecks. Some common causes of network bottlenecks are malfunctioning devices, having an excessive number of devices connected to the networks, limited bandwidth, and overcapacity for server utilisation.

Several considerations also need to be made when it comes to Internet connectivity, for example, the type of Internet services, Internet service providers, usage cost, and communication speed.

Mobile IoT devices in moving vehicles, require unique Internet connections, such as multi-service providers based on their current locations. For example, a device moving in Europe may require Internet connectivity from a French Internet Service Provider when it is in France and from a German Internet Service Provider when it is in Germany.

Major IoT Concerns

The major IoT concerns revolve around security and privacy. IoT technologies are rapidly-changing, expanding and transforming to different functions and shapes; hence, IoT technologies can have a tremendous impact on security.

The conventional security solutions may not meet the requirements of newer solutions. We need fresh security approaches to address new risks, issues, and dependencies. A recent addition to IoT security is the integration of blockchain to create secure and reliable connections. Blockchain enables smart IoT devices to control, monitor, and automate using a secure and reliable approach.

Privacy is related to security. It is well-known that security risks can cause privacy issues. IoT privacy concerns are complicated due to their nature; that is, they vary from country to country and are not always overt or obvious.

Therefore, to begin with, as the IoT solution architects, we need to pay special attention to the privacy requirements. Then, applying architectural rigours, such as adding privacy concerns to the architectural assessment and applying stringent risk management and mitigation process can be very useful.

Chapter Summary and Key Points

The main benefit and value proposition of IoT comes from collecting an enormous amount of data from various means and devices and then building services based on analyses of these massive amounts of data.

IoT devices generate massive amounts of data on an ongoing basis. These data sets go to the full data management life cycle.

The monitoring of IoT devices also creates a tremendous amount of data.

IoT Cloud is a crucial player in the ecosystem. The central

role the Cloud plays in IoT is to facilitate the data integration of the solution components.

Without the Cloud, the IoT can hardly add any value due to its real-time data and information-rich nature.

Edge computing can do the filtering for the Cloud to focus on the usable data.

IoT Analytics can also be provided as a consumption-based service. For example, AWS IoT Analytics is a fully-managed IoT analytics service that collects, pre-processes, enriches, stores and analyses IoT device data.

The speed of using clean data (aggregated in a single place) for analytics can help discover ways to reduce operational costs and increase the quality of ingested data. This is achieved by using an IoT based data lake.

The most common architectural challenges for IoT are mobility, scalability, capacity, extendibility, interoperability, network bottlenecks, and connectivity.

IoT Solutions certainly require comprehensive scalability and capacity plans.

IoT technologies are rapidly-changing, expanding and transforming to different functions and shapes; hence, IoT technologies can have a tremendous impact on security.

Chapter 6: Conclusions

We reached the final chapter. In this chapter, I provide conclusive remarks and critical considerations for the use of IoT and Cloud Computing services for Big Data and Analytics solutions by bringing all considerations together.

We covered that IoT, Big Data and Cloud Computing are three distinct technology domains with overlapping use cases. Each technology has its own merits; however, the combination of three creates a synergy and the golden opportunity for businesses to reap the exponential benefits. This combination can create technological magic for innovation when adequately architected, designed, implemented, and operated.

Integrating Big Data Analytics with IoT and Cloud architecture models can provide substantial business benefits. It is like a perfect match with triangulated integration. More specifically, IoT collects real-time data using smart objects. Big Data and Analytics solutions optimise data management solutions and present them with compelling business insights. Cloud collects, hosts, computes, stores, disseminates, make data available rapidly and economically in the overall ecosystem.

Big Data solutions without Cloud can be costly and complicated due to underlying infrastructure requirements for storage, process, and analytics. Not only the enormous volume of the Big Data but also other vital characteristics such as a variety of data sources, velocity, the integrity of data and required value from data in motion makes it a very complex system.

Data Architecture is the process of manipulating data and data sources from a current state to future state using established architectural frameworks. As Big Data architects, we use a top-down approach to start the solution description and use a bottom-up approach to maintain technical accuracy.

I pointed out that the critical attributes of Big Data are volume, velocity, variety, veracity, and value. Even though architecturally similar to traditional data, due to these complicated and interrelated attributes, Big Data and Analytics require innovative techniques, robust technology stacks, newer methods, and tools to deal with a massive amount of data.

I introduced the primary data analytics approaches, namely descriptive, predictive, prescriptive, and diagnostic. The descriptive analytics deals with situations such as what is happening right now based on incoming data. To recap, the predictive analytics refers to what might happen in the future. Prescriptive analytics deals with actions to be taken — the diagnostic analytics questions why something happened.

Understanding and being accountable for the nine phases of Big Data life cycle is essential for solution architects. These phases are Foundations, Acquisition, Preparation, Input, Processing, Output and Interpretation, Storage, Integration, Analytics, Consumption, Retention, Backup, Archival, and Destruction.

At a fundamental level, knowing the data types such as structured, semi-structured and unstructured, and choosing the right techniques, methods, tools and practices to work with them can be our daily solution tasks.

As principle-oriented professionals, solution architects need to be aware of national and international governance schemes and mandated principles by these schemes. We discussed the GDPR principles, including lawfulness, fairness, transparency, purpose limitation, data minimisation, accuracy, storage limitations, integrity, confidentiality, and accountability.

Focusing on data quality and knowing the essential data quality factors such as completeness, uniqueness, currency and conformance are critical success factors in creating high-quality solutions. The Big Data and Analytics governance system need to consider critical factors such as security, privacy, trust, operability, conformance, agility, innovation, and transformation of data.

As Big Data architects, we not only think in terms of the architectural or technical aspects of the data lifecycle but also think in business, entrepreneurial and strategic terms. Even though this book is based on the technical and architectural premise, we also emphasised the importance of business and strategy as Big Data and Analytics are business-driven disciplines. We use Big Data and Analytics to gain insights and make quick business decisions, reduce the cost for a product or service, test new markets to create new products, and services, and stay competitive in the market.

There is a trend to use semantic data analysis as part of the Big Data and Analytics solutions. Semantic data analysis can be used to create new meanings from unstructured data, especially in text format. The semantic approach is a growing aspect of Big Data. One of the recent growing text analytics technique is sentiment analysis, which is common in online social settings.

Even though Big Data is new from an architectural and technological perspective, there are many tools, methods, techniques, and patterns are evolving rapidly. It is imperative that we understand the state of art technology stacks, evolving products, tools, and services.

When we talk about the importance of clean raw data, we covered a key point called data lakes. In the simplest terms, data lakes are dynamically clean and instantly useable data sources made available for specific purposes. Use of data lakes helps the business stakeholders to identify opportunities quickly, make informed decisions, and act on their decision rapidly for speed to the market. Creating data lakes in Cloud is not only economical but also more accessible, more secure, more reliable, and agile for faster deployments.

There are many concerns related to the quality and accessibility of data in large organisations. There is a term coined to represent the inaccessibility of data. It is called data swamps. This term refers to an unmanaged data lake that may not be accessible by the intended consumers or may not provide desired business value.

We also mentioned data puddles and data ponds. Data puddle is a purpose-built data platform for a relatively smaller volume of data usually used by a specific single team mission. Data ponds can resemble a data warehouse designed for Big Data processing.

Even though data lakes are most commonly used for Big Data, there are still essential use cases for a classical data warehouse. A data warehouse can include optimised databases for analysis of relational data coming from enterprise applications and transactional enterprise systems.

Big Data solutions require heterogeneous technology and tools to fit the purpose. There is no single technology or tool which can fit all-purpose for developing Big Data solutions. Creating these tools, integrating them, hosting and supporting can be extremely expensive. There are still some organisations following this traditional path due to some constraints and compelling reasons such as security and regulatory compliance. However, many companies made new technology strategies to move their Big Data to Cloud and use Cloud-based services for Big Data solutions.

One of the primary reasons we move to Cloud services for the Big Data solutions is scalability and extensibility requirements met by Cloud's elasticity attribute. Maintaining scalability is critical for Big Data solutions.

We know that the use of open-source software and tools are critical to our Big Data solutions. They are instrumental, economical, agile and widely available. However, as solution architects, we should consider mixing open source and commercial systems based on their applicability and meeting our solution requirements. There may be exceptional regulatory requirements in using open-source software and tools; hence, this needs to be considered case by case for our solutions.

We learned the importance of data optimisation for Big Data solutions. We covered life cycle management. One of the critical aspects of the life cycle is data ingestion, which is the process of importing, transferring, loading processing and storing data for use. In terms of optimisation, we learnt that even though sharding can be a necessary technique, we need to use it with caution.

When we look at the Cloud service model, I emphasised a few key points. The cloud service model can expand or reduce computer resources based on service requirements. The Cloud services are provided on-demand and consumption-based pay as you go model. Cloud workloads can easily be moved from one location to another. This is an ideal use case for Big Data and Analytics.

We covered that the Cloud services are based on three major service models. IaaS (Infrastructure as a Service), PaaS (Platform as a Service) and SaaS (Software as a Service). However, we learnt that for our Big Data solution requirements, the essential Cloud service could be BDaaS (Big Data as a Service). BDaaS is a new Cloud-based service for Big Data solutions. Speed to market for Big Data solutions is crucial for competitive advantage in business. The cloud service model, especially using the BDaaS, is ideal to meet this critical business challenge and requirement.

Knowing the use cases for Cloud service model is critical for Big Data solution architects. We covered private, public, and hybrid models for Cloud services. Public Cloud is suitable and commonly used by small and medium-sized businesses, start-up companies and individuals, especially for Big Data solutions. The primary use case for private Cloud is security and regulatory compliance. Hybrid Cloud is a combination of private and public, and there may be a need to use all Cloud service models for our Big Data solutions.

From an architectural point of view, we learnt that APIs (Application Programming Interfaces) are critical to

IoT, Big Data and Cloud ecosystem. APIs are part of the IoT, Cloud and Big Data ecosystem to allow secure connections to the consumers, channels and other IoT, Cloud and Big Data applications. The most useful web services API is called Rest shorten from Restful.

We covered important architectural and business considerations related to IoT. We learned that the main benefit and value proposition of IoT comes from collecting an enormous amount of data from various means and devices and then building services based on analyses of these massive amounts of data. One of the relationships with Big Data and IoT is that IoT devices generate massive amounts of data on an ongoing basis. These data sets go to the full data management life cycle. Even monitoring of IoT devices for support purposes can create a tremendous amount of data.

IoT is also related to Cloud services. We understand that IoT Cloud is a critical player in the ecosystem. The primary role the Cloud plays in the IoT ecosystem is to facilitate the data integration of the solution components. Without the Cloud, the IoT can hardly add any value due to its real-time data and information-rich nature. Edge computing for IoT solutions can perform the filtering process for the Cloud to focus on the analytics of usable data.

IoT Analytics can also be provided as a consumption-based service. For example, AWS IoT Analytics is a fully-managed IoT analytics service that collects, pre-processes, enriches, stores and analyses IoT device data. The speed of using clean data (aggregated in a single place) for analytics can help discover ways to reduce operational costs and increase the quality of ingested data. We can achieve this goal by using IoT based data lakes in our Big Data solutions.

The most common architectural challenges for IoT are mobility, scalability, capacity, extendibility, interoperability, network bottlenecks, and connectivity. IoT Solutions certainly require overall scalability and capacity plans. IoT technologies are rapidly-changing, expanding and transforming to different functions and shapes; hence, IoT technologies can have a tremendous impact on security and privacy.

As a last but not the least critical point, security is not only critical for IoT, but it is vital for Big Data coming from various sources; and particularly imperative for Cloud services hosted across different time zones. This means that a solution architect working on Big Data solutions using IoT and Cloud must be extremely security-aware and capable of governing the security requirements and obligations by delegating them for the deepest granular level of details with multiple subject matter experts in an integrated way. We must be super alert not to compromise security despite all complications when dealing with the triangulated use of IoT, Big Data, and Cloud services.

Appendix

List of Commercial Big Data and Analytics Tools, Technologies and Platforms

As mentioned in the commercial tools section, I provide this list for awareness and information purposes only. This is not an exhaustive list. It covers only the most widely and frequently used products and services.

I sorted out the list alphabetically to make it easy to remember them or find them when needed. As this book is technology and vendor agnostic, no assessment made for any commercial products.

I highly recommend to make your assessment of these products based on unique requirements and use cases of your solutions, in addition to the commercial and financial situation of your funding organisation.

1010data

Actian Analytics Platform

Amazon Web Services

Amdocs Insight

Arcadia Data

Attivio Active Intelligence Engine

BigObject

BlueTalon

Celebrus Technologies

Cisco Bigdata

Cloudera Enterprise Bigdata

CSC Big Data Platform

Datameer

DataStax Bigdata

DataTorrent

Dell Bigdata Analytics

FICO Big Data Analyzer

Flytxt

GE Industrial Internet

GoodData

Google BigQuery and Bigdata

Guavus

Hortonworks Data Platform

HP Bigdata

HPCC Systems Big Data

IBM BigData

Informatica PowerCenter Big Data Edition

Intel Bigdata

Kognitio Analytical Platform

MapR Converged Data Platform

Microsoft Azure

MicroStrategy Bigdata

Mu Sigma Bigdata

Next Pathway

Opera Solutions Bigdata

Opera Solutions Signal Hub

Opera Solutions Signal Hubs

Oracle Bigdata Analytics

Pachyderm

Palatir Bigdata

Pentaho Big Data Analytics

Periscope Data

Pivotal Bigdata

Qubole

Rubikloud

SAP Bigdata Analytics

SGI Bigdata

Splunk Bigdata Analytics.

Syncsort

Teradata Bigdata Analytics.

VMware

Wavefront

Other Books in This Series

A Modern Enterprise Architecture Approach Empowered with Mobility, Cloud, IoT & Big Data

Modernise and transform the enterprise with pragmatic architecture, powerful technologies, innovative agility, and fusion

I authored this book to provide essential guidance, compelling ideas, and unique ways to Enterprise Architects so that they can successfully perform complex enterprise modernisation initiatives transforming from chaos to coherence. This is not an ordinary theory book describing Enterprise Architecture in detail. There are myriad of books on the market and in libraries discussing details of enterprise architecture.

As a practising Senior Enterprise Architect myself, I read hundreds of those books and articles to learn different views. They have been valuable to me to establish my foundations in the earlier phase of my profession. However, what is missing now is a concise guidance book showing Enterprise Architects the novel approaches, insights from the real-life experience and experimentations, and pointing out the differentiating technologies for enterprise modernisation. If only there were such a guide when I started engaging in modernisation and transformation programs.

The biggest lesson learned is the business outcome

of the enterprise modernisation. What genuinely matters for business is the return on investment of the enterprise architecture and its monetising capabilities. The rest is the theory because nowadays sponsoring executives, due to economic climate, have no interest, attention, or tolerance for non-profitable ventures. I am sorry for disappointing some idealistic Enterprise Architects, but with due respect, it is the reality, and we cannot change it. This book deals with reality rather than theoretical perfection. Anyone against this view on this climate must be coming from another planet.

In this concise, uncluttered and easy-to-read book, I attempt to show the significant pain points and valuable considerations for enterprise modernisation using a structured approach. The architectural rigour is still essential. We cannot compromise the rigour aiming to the quality of products and services as a target outcome. However, there must be a delicate balance among architectural rigour, business value, and speed to market. I applied this pragmatic approach to multiple substantial transformation initiatives and complex modernisations programs. The key point is using an incrementally progressing iterative approach to every aspect of modernisation initiatives, including people, processes, tools, and technologies as a whole.

Starting with a high-level view of enterprise architecture to set the context, I provided a dozen of distinct chapters to point out and elaborate on the factors which can make a real difference in dealing with complexity and producing excellent modernisation initiatives. As eminent leaders, Enterprise Architects are the critical talents who can undertake this massive mission using their people and technology skills, in addition to many critical attributes such as calm and composed approach. They are architects, not firefighters. I have full confidence that this book can provide valuable insights and aha moments for these talented architects to tackle this enormous mission turning chaos to coherence.

A Practical Guide for IoT Solution Architects

Architecting secure, agile, economic, highly available, well-performing IoT ecosystems

The focus of this book is to provide IoT solution architects with practical guidance and a unique perspective. Solution architects working in IoT ecosystems have an unprecedented level of responsibility at work; therefore, dealing with IoT ecosystems can be daunting.

As an experienced practitioner of this topic, I understand the challenges faced by the IoT solution architects. In this book, I have reflected upon my insights based on my solution architecture experience spread across three decades. In addition, this book can also guide other architects and designers who want to learn the architectural aspects of IoT and understand the key challenges and practical resolutions in IoT solution architectures. Each chapter focuses on the key aspects that form the framing scope for this book; namely, security, availability, performance, agility, and cost-effectiveness.

In this book, I have also provided useful definitions, a brief practical background on IoT and a guiding chapter on solution architecture development. The content is mainly practical; hence, it can be applied or be a supplemental input to the architectural projects at hand.

A Technical Excellence Framework for Innovative Digital Transformation Leadership

Transform enterprise with technical excellence, innovation, simplicity, agility, fusion, and collaboration

The primary purpose of this book is to provide valuable insights for digital transformational leadership empowered by technical excellence by using a pragmatic five-pillar framework. This empowering framework aims to help the reader understand the common characteristics of technical and technology leaders in a structured way.

Even though there are different types of leaders in broad-spectrum engaging in digital transformations, in this book, we only concentrate on excellent technical and technology leaders having digital transformation goals to deal with technological disruptions and robust capabilities to create new revenue streams. No matter whether these leaders may hold formal executive titles or just domain specialist titles, they demonstrate vital characteristics of excellent technical leadership capabilities enabling them to lead complex and complicated digital transformation initiatives.

The primary reason we need to understand technical excellence and required capabilities for digital transformational leadership in a structured context is to model their attributes and transfer the well-known characteristics to the aspiring leaders and the next generations. We can transfer our understanding of these capabilities at an individual level and apply them to our day to day activities. We can even turn them into useful habits to excel in our professional goals. Alternatively, we can pass this information to other people that we are responsible for, such as our teenagers aiming for digital leadership roles, tertiary students, mentees, and colleagues.

We attempt to define the roles of strategic technical and technology leaders using a specific framework, based on innovation, simplicity, agility, collaboration, fusion and technical excellence. This framework offers a common understanding of the critical factors of the leader. The structured analysis presented in this book can be valuable to understand the contribution of technical leaders clearly.

Admittedly, this book has a bias towards the positive attributes of excellent leaders on purpose. The compelling reason for this bias is to focus on the positive aspects and describe these attributes concisely in an adequate amount to grasp the topic so that these positive attributes can be reused and modelled by the aspiring leaders. As the other side of the coin is also essential for different insights, I plan to deal with the detrimental aspects of useless leaders in a separate book, perhaps under the lessons learned context considering different use cases for a different audience type. Consequently, I excluded the negative aspects of useless leaders in this book.

Digital Intelligence

A framework to digital transformation capabilities

I authored this book because dealing with intelligence, and the digital world is a passion for me and wanted to share my passion with you. In this book, I aim to provide compelling ideas and unique ways to increase, enhance, and deepen your digital intelligence and awareness and apply them to your organisation's digital journey particularly for modernisation and transformation initiatives. I used the architectural thinking approach as the primary framework to convey my message.

Based on my architectural thought leadership on various digital transformation and modernisation engagements, with the accumulated wealth of knowledge and skills, I want to share these learnings in a concise book hoping to add value by contributing to the broader digital community and the progressing initiatives.

Rest assured, this is not a theory or an academic book. It is purely practical and based on lessons learned from real enterprise transformation and modernisation initiatives taken in large corporate environments. I made every effort to make this book concise, uncluttered, and easy-to-read by removing technical jargons for a broader audience who want to enhance digital intelligence and awareness.

Upfront, this book is not about a tool, application, a single product, specific technology, or service, and certainly not to endorse any of these items. However, this book focuses on architectural thinking and methodical approach to improve digital intelligence and awareness. It is not like typical digital transformation books available on the market. In this book, I do not cover and repeat the same content of those books describing digital transformations.

My purpose is different. What distinguishes this book from other books is that I provide an innovative thinking framework and a methodical approach to increase your digital quotient based on experience, aiming not to sell or endorse any products or services even though I mention some prominent technologies which enable digital transformation, for your digital awareness, intelligence, and capabilities.

Architecting Digital Transformation

12-step Architectural Leadership Method

Enterprises are facing enormous challenges to respond to the rapid changes and growing demands of digital consumers globally. There is constant search to find solutions to the growing problems. The most optimal solution to address this problem is to architect our enterprise digital transformation requirements aligning with digital trends and innovative frameworks as described in this book with an articulated 12-step method.

Architecting digital transformations address the root causes of fundamental issues that we experience in the digital world. The proliferation of digital media in the form of images, sound, and videos created a massive demand for our infrastructure to scale globally. Relentless sharing of these media types creates an unsustainable load over the networks, applications, and other expensive infrastructure components unless an effective capacity plan is in place.

Based on my architectural thought leadership on various enterprise architecture initiatives, digital transformation, and modernisation engagements, with my accumulated body of knowledge and skills from practical settings, I want to share these learnings in a concise book with a specific 12-step method hoping to add value by contributing to the broader digital community and the progressing digital transformation initiatives.

I made every effort to make this book concise, uncluttered, and easy-to-read by removing technical jargons to make it readable by a broader audience who want to architect their digital transformation programs to align with the growing demands of their digital consumers.

In this book, I highlight the problems from an architectural point of view, following established and emerging methods, and recommend effective solutions to address them in a methodical way.

What distinguishes this book from other books on the market is that I provide a practical framework and a methodical approach to architect your organisation's digital infrastructure, applications, data, security, and other components based on experience, aiming not to sell or endorse any products or services to you.

About the Author

Dr Mehmet Yildiz is a Distinguished Enterprise Architect L3 certified from the Open Group. Working in the IT industry over the last 35 years, he recently focuses on cutting edge technology solutions, such as IoT, Blockchain, Cognitive, Cloud, Fog, and Edge Computing. He is a hands-on practitioner for solution architectures leading complex corporate projects and an Agile champion. As an innovation evangelist in all walks of life, he is also a recognised inventor. Mehmet teaches the best architectural practices at work, mentors his colleagues, supervises doctoral students, and provides industry-level lectures to postgraduate students at several universities in Australia. You can contact the author from his author platform https://digitalmehmet.com